COWLEY PUBLICATIONS *is a ministry of the brothers of the Society of Saint John the Evangelist, a monastic order in the Episcopal Church. Our mission is to provide books and resources for those seeking spiritual and theological formation.* COWLEY PUBLICATIONS *is committed to developing a new generation of writers and teachers who will encourage people to think and pray in new ways about spirituality, reconciliation, and the future.*

*Falling in Love
with God*

Falling in Love with God:

Passion, Prayer, and the Song of Songs

TARA SOUGHERS

Let him kiss me with the kisses of his mouth!
(Song of Songs 1:2)

Cowley Publications
Cambridge, Massachusetts

Published in the United States of America by Cowley Publications, a division of the Society of Saint John the Evangelist. No portion of this book may be reproduced, stored in or introduced into a retrieval system, or transmitted, in any form or by any means—including photocopying—without the prior written permission of Cowley Publications, except in the case of brief quotations embedded in critical articles and reviews.

Library of Congress Cataloging-in-Publication Data

Soughers, Tara, 1961-
    Falling in love with God : passion, prayer, and the Song of Songs / Tara Soughers.
        p. cm.
    Includes bibliographical references.
    ISBN 1-56101-264-5 (pbk. : alk. paper)   1. Bible. O.T. Song of Solomon—Devotional use. 2. Bible. O.T. Song of Solomon—Commentaries.   I. Title.
    BS1485.54.S68 2005
    242'.5--dc22

                                                                    2004026647

Scripture quotations are taken from The New Revised Standard Version of the Bible, © 1989, by the Division of Christian Education of the National Council of the Churches of Christ in the United States of America. Used by permission.

Cover design by Gary Ragaglia
Interior design and typesetting by Andrew MacBride

This book was printed in the United States of America on acid-free paper.

Cowley Publications
4 Brattle Street
Cambridge, Massachusetts 02138
800-225-1534 • www.cowley.org

CONTENTS

ACKNOWLEDGMENTS

To fully live out our faith, we need a community. In order to grow in our relationship with God, we need the support and companionship of others. I have found that such a community is also required to write a book. It is perhaps dangerous to thank those who served in that role for this book, for I risk leaving someone out. Not to thank them, however, would be to deny the blessings that God has showered upon me.

First of all, I would like to thank my family, who remained supportive even as I was working during vacations. I thank my children, Arielle and Gregory, who never doubted that the book would be published. I am grateful to my husband, Michael Dehn, who spent many hours helping to polish the manuscript for submission.

I also want to thank Gloria Schultz of the Portland, Connecticut Public Library, who spent a great deal of effort tracking down unusual references through the interlibrary loan system. Our public libraries are one of our greatest assets.

The idea of for this book begin with a course offered by the Shalem Institute, and I will always be grateful for the role that course played in the reflections in this book. I thank Rev. Anne Kimball, my spiritual advisor, who first described my sometimes tumultuous spiritual life as a love affair with God, and whose words led me to explore the Song of Songs.

The book was strengthened by the comments of Rev. Tilden Edwards, Rev. Dr. Laura Ahrens, and Rev. Edward Coolidge. The discussions I had with them, and their support, were invaluable.

Last, I want to thank Michael Wilt, editorial director of Cowley Publications, and Ulrike Guthrie. Their editorial suggestions made the melody sing more clearly.

For these and all the blessings of community, I give thanks to God.

Chapter

Introduction

> I adjure you, O daughters of Jerusalem,
>> by the gazelles or the wild does:
> do not stir up or awaken love
>> until it is ready!
>> *(2:7)*

Passion and love are dangerous things! Make sure you are ready before you stir them up! The warning is sounded multiple times in the Song of Songs, and has been heard—but perhaps a little too well.

The Song of Songs is almost unknown to most readers of the Bible. Rarely is it read in church. Its unabashed sensuality makes it an embarrassment in most church settings. Most people tend to forget it even exists. Hidden between the larger books of Ecclesiastes and Isaiah, it is rare even to happen upon it. In fact, the only part I remembered hearing with any regularity over the years was the small section (8:6–7) that is sometimes used at weddings. Occasionally a line or two would be quoted in other contexts, and I would be reminded again of its beauty.

I never completely forgot it was there, but until recently I did not think much about the Song of Songs either. Several years ago, however, I began to get drawn more deeply into contemplative prayer. It seemed to nurture and feed my soul in new ways. I became curious about others who had followed this path, and the search led me to some of the medieval mystics.

I found their erotic imagery (often based on the Song of Songs) disturbing at first. Were the mystics mentally unbalanced? I speculated on the connection between their erotic longings for God and the celibacy to which they were avowed. I wondered if it was something peculiar to that age. In any case, I dismissed such imagery as something likely never to have any meaning for me. However, as I have found out over and over again through-out my spiritual life, it is dangerous to say never.

A few years later at a retreat, I again experienced a change in my perspective. I had been picturing Jesus as a close friend, a playmate. I had been relaxing in a rather joyful sense of Christ's presence with me. In the midst of an extended time of quiet, I suddenly felt as though I had been hit with a ton of bricks. What had felt like a warm friendship suddenly became much more in-tense. I began to experience some of what the mystics had meant about God's passionate longing for us.

Luckily, at that conference I had also picked up a copy of Janet Ruffing's book *Spiritual Direction: Beyond the Beginnings*. In it she talks about the use of romantic imagery in our relation-ship with God. She also talks about how difficult it is for people in the modern world to allow themselves to be drawn into what seems to be a strange world, one known primarily by medieval monastic mystics. With her encouragement I allowed myself to experience a new and startlingly different way of relating to God.[1]

In the year following the retreat, I found myself returning often to the Song of Songs to remember, to re-experience, but most of all, to help me put words to experiences that did not fall in the "normal, ordinary" realm. The images in that book al-lowed me to give voice to my growing longing for God, and to experience a sense of God's incredible longing for me. That ex-perience revealed new depths in my understanding of God, and it revealed new insights about myself. Only love has the power to shake our foundations and place us on a new and higher ground. By falling in love, I was transformed, and my relation-ship to God will never be the same.

I write this book, not as an expert on praying or even as an expert in the Song of Songs, but as someone who has been led into a more passionate relationship with God, thanks to this text. The words of the Song have become my words of prayer. When John of the Cross was induced by Madre Ana de Jesus to write a commentary on his *Spiritual Canticle,* he began the introduction with the words, "These stanzas, Reverend Mother, were obviously composed with a certain burning love of God."[2] I hope the same will be said of this work.

I invite you to stick your toes into this stream of spiritual water, a stream with a long tradition. I invite you to consider how to express your own longing for God and how to experience God's longing for you. Not everyone will find this way of expressing his or her desires helpful, but it may be that God is waiting to speak to you through the voice of the bridegroom.

I have become convinced that each of us has a deep longing and desire for God. Pascal called it a God-shaped hole within, that nothing else can ever truly fill.

The Song of Songs has reminded me that God also has a deep longing for each one of us. We are incredibly beautiful and precious in God's eyes, and in loving us, God has given us a surprising amount of influence over God's self! Although the initiative in the relationship is God's, the use of the image of a romantic relationship reminds us that love is at its best when it is mutual.

Praying is a dangerous business, for through it God desires to transform us into something more. God desires to draw us more fully into God's life, to be fully and completely God's. Any prayer, therefore, has an element of risk.

Praying the Song is indeed a risky business, for it asks God to send us head over heels in love. It seeks to awaken our desire for God, which cares little for proprieties. It seeks to help us experience God's passionate desire for us, a desire that wants to claim us exclusively for God.

So come and pray the Song of Songs with me. But be warned that you do so at your own risk. For God will not in the end be satisfied with anything short of your passionate love. It is a love that God awakens in us as a response to God's passionate love for us.

Falling in love is not for the fainthearted, as lovers through the centuries can attest.

Chapter

*Praying
with the
Song of
Songs
Through
the Ages*

*I advise and counsel everyone who is not yet rid of the
vexations of flesh and blood and has not ceased to feel
the passion of his bodily nature, to refrain completely
from reading this little book and the things that will
be said about it.*[3]

Origen had definite ideas about who should or should not read the
Song of Songs, and in some ways, his reservations have been shared
by many Church leaders in the centuries since his time. The Song
has proven to be a difficult problem for the religious communities
that honor and treasure the Hebrew Scriptures. It is a part of the
canon—the accepted books of holy writings that are definitive for
both Jews and Christians—and so cannot be easily dismissed. Nevertheless, its intense sensuality, unmatched in biblical literature,
has been an embarrassment. Its proclamation of the importance
of passionate love in our relationship with God surprises and even
startles us. The writer Madeleine L'Engle laments that although
the Song contains the strongest language we have about love, it
appears nowhere in the Episcopal lectionary (the prescribed course
of Bible readings).[4] Its unadorned sensuality is seen as appropriate only for weddings nowadays, and even then the choice of verses
is small. In contrast, in the Middle Ages, the Song was the most
quoted book of Scripture.[5]

Of course, weddings might be one of the most appropriate
uses for the Song of Songs. Indeed, millennia after the compo-
sition of the Song, similar hymns of praise were used in Middle
Eastern weddings. The custom of singing *wasf,* songs of praise
about the bride's or groom's body, was a part of wedding celebra-
tions through at least the eighteenth century in Arabian villages.
As a part of the celebration, the bride would also dance with a
sword while describing her own beauty. During the weeklong
wedding festivities, the bride and groom would be treated as a

king and queen, and more songs extolling the "queen's" beauty
would be sung.[6]

The form of the Song of Songs seems to follow a similar tradition, but that does not explain why this book was preserved as
sacred Scripture when other love poetry was not. Part of the answer is that it was attributed to a well-known biblical figure: King
Solomon. The other element is its surprising interpretive history, in which the Song became an allegory of human-divine
love. Whether it is human love poetry or an allegory of divine
love, the Song of Songs has been able to hold both meanings in
tension. According to Carey Ellen Walsh, the Song's interpretive history has bounced from one extreme to another:

> First the Song of Songs has suffered from a unique interpre-
> tative history, where it was considered either too sensual
> and so it was made an allegory about religion, or merely sex-
> ual and it was left at that. The scholarly literature on the
> Song has vacillated from one extreme to the other and be-
> trays an interpretive confusion that I wanted to address.[7]

This book does not trace the Song's entire long and varied
history of interpretation. Yet because it is helpful to have some
sense of its history, as a context for this book, I will provide a
short overview of that history before we plunge into our study
of the Song.

🖾 A Short Interpretive History of the Song of Songs
Jewish Meanings

The first to propose an allegorical interpretation of the Song
was Rabbi Akiva. Rabbi Akiva, spiritual leader of the Jewish re-
bellion in 135 CE, is still the most revered and quoted of all
Torah scholars. For him the Song of Songs was not simply something added to God's word; it was, in fact, the heart of it. He
spoke of the Song of Songs as the Scriptures' inner sanctum. Its

role in the Scriptures was analogous to the Holy of Holies within the Jerusalem Temple.[8]

The idea of comparing the love of the people of Israel and God to that of a husband and wife is not unique to the Song. In fact, such imagery is used throughout the prophetic books. What is unusual in the Song is the detail in which the relationship is explored and the passion (implied, perhaps, but not described in the other biblical books) that is celebrated. For Rabbi Akiva, the love between Israel and God was called to rise to that level of passion, and he declared "that the whole world realized its supreme purpose only on the day when the Song of Songs was given to Israel."[9]

Not all Jews shared Rabbi Akiva's enthusiasm for the Song. More conservative elements often found its unbridled sensuality troubling and feared that it might corrupt the young. Ancient Jewish tradition taught that one should read the Song only after the age of thirty and after one had read the rest of the canon.[10] Presumably only then would it not lead to improper thoughts.

In later Jewish mystical tradition, the allegorical element of the interpretation was developed further. The Zohar, a mystical commentary on the Pentateuch from the late thirteenth century, claimed that the Song of Songs revealed something about the nature of God. It argued that the intercourse between the male and female aspects of God could be influenced by human sexual relations such as described in the Song of Songs.[11] Already the many and varied possibilities inherent in an allegorical interpretation are becoming evident.

Early Christian Meanings

Christian commentators had similar struggles with the Song of Songs (or the Canticle of Canticles, as it was often known). Though recognizing in the Song something vital to the faith, they worried about its effect on those who were not properly prepared for its spiritual message. Origen, one of the earliest

Christian commentators, cautioned that one should not read the Song of Songs until the person not only had read Proverbs and Ecclesiastes (the other books attributed to Solomon) but also had fully incorporated their messages into her or his life:

> This book comes last that a man may come to it when his manner of life has been purified and he has learnt to know the difference between things corruptible and things incorruptible; so that nothing in the metaphors used to describe and represent the love of the Bride for her celestial Bridegroom—that is of the perfect soul for the Word of God—may cause him to stumble. For, when the soul has completed these studies, by means of which it is cleansed in all its actions and habits and is led to discriminate between natural things, it is competent to proceed to dogmatic and mystical matters, and in this way advances to the contemplation of the Godhead with pure and spiritual love.[12]

Many Christian commentators followed the Jewish tradition of interpreting the Song allegorically. From the time of Origen through the Middle Ages, the two most favored interpretations for the person of the bride were as either the individual soul or the Church. The bride as the Church was perhaps the one most favored by those trying to make the Song serve more communal purposes, but the mystics have usually understood the bride as the individual soul.

For Origen, as for Rabbi Akiva, the Song of Songs was of profound importance. Like Rabbi Akiva, he saw the Song as an allegory of God's love. Origen is known to have written ten books of commentaries on the Canticle of Canticles as well as a number of sermons. (Unfortunately, much of his original work has been lost, although some still exists in later Latin translations.)

Origen acknowledged three different levels of meaning in the Song. The first was the direct and carnal sense. The second level of meaning referred to the marriage of Christ with the

Church. The third level referred to the union of the Logos (or Word) with the human soul.[13]

Although he deals with all those levels, it is clear from reading Origen's writings that the one closest to his heart is the second level. Actually, for him levels two and three are almost inseparable, for he believes that it is only through the Church that an individual soul can come to know Christ. "And what had been fulfilled in the Church as a result of her bridal union with Christ, the same is effected in every soul entering into bridal relations with Christ."[14]

Origen spends a great deal of effort translating the images in the Song into teachings appropriate for the Church. Much of the emphasis in his commentary is on the need for the bride (either Church or individual) to purify herself and to grow in moral virtue in order to become a fit bride for the groom. There is a strong ethical strand in Origen's interpretation of the work.

This leads Origen to see in the groom's description of her beauty a description not of the bride's physical beauty but of her moral stature. Cheeks become signs of her integrity, modesty, and chastity. The neck is a symbol of obedience.[15] The ointments that are used are symbolic of the Law and the prophets that guide her.[16] When the bride talks about the groom like a bag of myrrh between her breasts, her breast becomes the place of holy teachings.[17]

Origen takes an intellectual approach to the Song, analyzing the text for the knowledge it imparts. However, a line in his prologue hints that for all his insistence on treating it as an exercise in knowledge, Origen was not unfamiliar with the experience of passionate love for God. "And deeply indeed did she love Him, whether we take her as the soul made in His image, or as the Church."[18]

The Middle Ages

Like Origen, Bernard of Clairvaux spent a great deal of time studying the Song of Songs. During his tenure as abbot of

Clairvaux, Bernard preached a total of eighty-five sermons on this small book. For him, as for Rabbi Akiva, the Song was a means of encountering God. "It is clear that this work was not written by human wit, but was composed by the art of the Spirit. As a result, even if it is difficult to understand, it is nevertheless a source of delight to him who looks into it."[19]

The focus for Bernard is not on the Church, but on the individual soul and its response to Christ. Unlike Origen, his emphasis is not on growth in the knowledge of theology and the practice of virtue. Instead, he is urging his monks to grow in their love of and passion for God. "The teaching of the Spirit does not sharpen curiosity; it inspires love."[20]

In his penultimate sermon, Bernard sums up what the Song of Songs and his own experience of God have taught him. "I love, and I cannot doubt that I am loved, any more than that I love. Nor can I fear his face whose love I experienced."[21] In this ecstatic experience of God's presence and love, he sounds very much like a later medieval figure well known for his commentary, John of the Cross.

It was while he was imprisoned by his own religious order that John of the Cross wrote most of the verses of his *Spiritual Canticle*. The canticle is not a direct commentary on the Song of Songs. Instead it is a love poem to God, based on the imagery in the Song. In this work John affirms both the reality of darkness when the Lover seems absent and the blinding light of the Beloved when present.

John initially resisted entreaties to explain what he meant by his verses, preferring to allow the verses to speak for themselves. Later, however, John undertook with great reluctance to provide a brief commentary on his verses, and hence on his understanding of the Song of Songs on which his verses were based.

For John, the soul's relationship with God was characterized by passionate love. In his commentary he attempts to explain what seems to him to be beyond explanation. He has experienced a radical transformation of his soul, not by learning more about God but by being captured by God's love and giving himself fully, without reservation, to God until the two are united. Although John is clear that this union is a gift from God, he believes that it is Christ's will to give it to us once we have at last come to that state where barriers no longer exist between our Beloved and us. "The soul possessing nothing that might withhold her from God cannot remain long without a visit from the beloved."[22] In John of the Cross, the full passion of the Song of Songs was brought to bear upon the relationship of the individual with God.

Modern Times

Interpretation of the Song of Songs still continues to vacillate between two extremes: human love poetry and an allegory for God's love. In recent times allegorical interpretations have fallen out of favor. Instead studies that focus on its historical context or on it as a description of purely human love have predominated.

Raymond Jacques Tournay, in *Word of God: Song of Love,* focuses on the element of allegory, a surprising choice for a twentieth-century scholar. Tournay is much more interested, however, in the way the Song of Songs spoke to its immediate historical context than in its application to our times. In studying the Song, Tournay sees many elements that he believes are allegorical symbols of events in the life of King David. He sees in its veiled references a message of hope for the people of the Second Temple Period, who were waiting for a messiah.

> [T]he Song is a love poem oriented ultimately toward what was the supreme and invincible hope of the chosen people of the Second Temple period: the coming of the Messiah, at the same time a new David and a new Solomon awaited so anxiously by the daughter of Zion.[23]

Sidney Brichto, on the other hand, removes all allegorical elements, focusing almost exclusively on the Song as a drama. In the People's Bible, Brichto chooses to portray the Song as a love song about a king trying to win the love of a country girl (who is already in love with a shepherd).[24] This is not a new idea, and many earlier interpreters have assumed that the king in question is Solomon, an assumption that aims to solidify its historical context.

On the other hand, there are those commentators who rejoice in the fact that the Song is purely human love poetry, able to speak to us of human desire and passion. Bloch and Bloch's translation of the Song of Songs affirms their belief that the book's power comes from acknowledging the sacredness of human love.[25] Marcia Falk, in her translation, also rejoices in what can be learned about human relationships from the poetry, without resorting to the need for allegorical interpretations. "Read on the simplest level—without delving into allegory or elaborate hypotheses of structural or contextual unity—the Song reveals itself as a richly textured tapestry, woven from variegated strands of nuance and meaning."[26]

As the interpretive pendulum swings back and forth between the two extremes—human love poetry and allegory—Walsh suggests another way of viewing this work. Although she affirms that the Song of Songs is, at its most basic, a book about human desire, she believes that this glimpse into desire has much to teach us about life and about God:

> This book is about desire because it is the subject of this Song, and because it is the subject of life when we get right down to it. Spirituality, for example, is no hedged bet to soften the edges of a stressful life; still less is it marked solely by a lazy obedience to a tradition we just ended up inheriting. Instead, the spiritual quest is precisely—no more, and nothing less than—the yearning for meaning, the hungry desire for it, and just as important, the painful coping with its periodic absence. That we all search and work for more

meaning, for fuller lives during the course of our lives, makes of us all spiritual beings.[27]

Although I appreciate Walsh's view, I think there is more to the Song than she allows. Perhaps, in our descriptions of God and God's love, we can best start with human love. Human love and human passion can indeed be powerful forces. They are a reflection of the love that is at the heart of God. Love imagery can help us describe things and relationships that are indescribable.

I do not believe, however, that from such descriptions alone we can really comprehend the love of God. The love of God is something that has to be experienced first, before the words of the Song really begin to sing in our hearts. Because of that, this book is an invitation to pray with the Song. In praying we open ourselves to God's love so that the words of this love poem may come alive in us.

The Song may be interpreted in many ways. The best way is the one that brings you face to face with your Lover.

▨ Who Is the Bridegroom?

Throughout history there have been a number of answers to the question of the bride's identity. Some have championed the notion of the bride as standing for the individual soul or the Church. Others have held her to represent the Virgin Mary. Still other theories have held the bride to be Solomon's Egyptian princess or a peasant courted by Solomon.

The identity of the groom has been less in debate. Of those commentators who have seen in this book something beyond a mere description of human love, the male lover has usually been seen as God. Of course, the commentators have held to a different understanding of God depending on whether they were Jewish or Christian.

For me, the Lover in the Song is Christ. My spirituality has been formed and is continually nourished in the Christian tradition. When I seek my Beloved, it is Christ whom I seek.

In writing this book, however, I was aware that the Song of Songs has the potential to reach beyond those formed in the Christian or even the Judeo-Christian tradition. Most religious traditions of the world have their mystics, and romantic imagery is common to such seekers of God. In fact, it is often in the realm of direct experience with God that the world's religions find their closest connections. According to the Sufi poet and mystic Rumi, "Love is the astrolabe that sights into the mysteries of God."[28]

In writing this book, therefore, I have intentionally not used the name of Christ in the meditations or the suggested exercises. I have preferred to speak of the male character as the Groom or the Lover or even God. My hope is that it would make it easier for those who come from non-Christian traditions to explore a love relationship with the One who loves us, and who is known by many names. Feel free to substitute the name by which you know your Lover.

Gender in the Song of Songs

In previous centuries, men have felt comfortable describing themselves in feminine terms in relation to God. Women were considered the weaker, more passive, and subservient sex. All those characteristics were considered appropriate in the face of God's power and might, and that would explain the appeal of literature such as the Song of Songs to men such as Origen, Bernard, and John of the Cross. (A whole range of women mystics also found romantic imagery very important, although they seem to have been less likely to write commentaries on the Song of Songs.)

As a woman, I know that the feminine imagery for the primary character in the Song of Songs does make it easy for me to relate to it. According to Janet Ruffing, though, romantic God imagery can be more difficult for heterosexual men and homosexual women, due to the prevailing masculine imagery and the corresponding lack of feminine imagery for God in much of the biblical literature and in Church tradition.[29]

God as male is not necessarily inviting, however, even for heterosexual women. I know that it was the negative associations of such masculine imagery that made me initially resistant to the romantic imagery of the Song of Songs. I had no desire to be weak, passive, and subservient, qualities often assigned to women. I really wanted God to be someone who treated me as an adult.

The surprise in the Song of Songs is that the bride is neither weak, passive, nor subservient. She knows what she wants, and she goes out to get it. She is direct, in a culture that condemns such forwardness. She may be firmly held by her love, but the groom is equally captive. In fact, there is a surprising equality between the characters, a theme we will discuss more fully in chapter 18.

That equality may make it easier for men (and women) to relate to this work. What might it mean if God wants us, not as children or slaves, but as lovers and partners? Come and find out.

Using This Book

Chapters 3 through 17 contain meditations on the Song of Songs, and each chapter follows a consistent format. The first part of each chapter is devoted to commentary on a portion of the Song. That part is further divided into three smaller sections to allow us to savor each piece of this short work.

At the beginning of each section, the portion of the Song of Songs that will be discussed is printed. I invite you to read through it several times, listening for what the text might be saying to you, before reading the commentary. There is an added richness in such a dialogue. The commentary on the verses is meant not to be exhaustive, but evocative. I comment on what has had meaning for me as I have prayed these passages, but Scripture is endlessly rich. It may be that different facets of the same passage strike you. Let the Spirit lead you to what you need to hear.

At the end of each chapter are suggested journal exercises and prayer forms. I invite you to read through them and to see which, if any, you feel drawn to explore further. The journal exercises contain questions that have arisen for me in living with the passages. Do not feel that you need to do all the exercises listed, for we do not all have the same questions. If other questions arise, trust that God is leading you where you need to go.

The prayer forms continue the themes raised in the commentary, and they often contain silence, because it was through contemplative prayer that this book came alive for me. People have varying needs for and tolerances for silence. I have not suggested an amount of time for the meditations; I think the optimal time of silence is something you will need to explore for yourself.

If your prayer life has little silence, I encourage you to try to incorporate some into it. The thought of sitting in silence can be quite intimidating, but the fruits can be rich. If you are not used to silence, I recommend that you begin with only short periods of silence, perhaps five to ten minutes. Even that, at first, can seem incredibly long. As you begin to relax into the silence, however, it may be possible to gradually lengthen the time.

If you want to incorporate silence in your prayer life, it is best to find a place that is relatively quiet, where you will not be interrupted. Don't worry if you get distracted as you pray; everyone does. Distractions are a part of being human. If you find thoughts intruding upon your silence, gently let them go, and return to whatever you are using to focus your prayers. Getting upset with yourself about becoming distracted will only prolong the disruption. I suggest that you try several times before you decide that silence is not for you. It can take some time to quiet our busy minds. Sometimes it is easier to be silent if you can find others to share the silence with you.

Silence can, I think, open us up to experience God in a different way. It can free us of some of our need to be in control. It can still our minds and hearts, allowing us to listen more deeply for the whisper of God's word. It can engage our imaginations and our hearts in new and freer ways.

Such freedom and creativity can flow out of other activities as well. For some people, dance or art can open up new ways of relating to God. Experiment with what works well for you. As you do so, consider the support and nurture that you will need to deepen your relationship with God. After all, humans are not meant to be alone, but to be in community with others. A spiritual friend or director can also support, nurture, and challenge us as we explore new ways of being in relationship with God. Lovers need to talk of their love with others!

I think that the power of the Song of Songs lies not in its theology (although it is theological) but in its passion for God. It has, I think, been neglected throughout the centuries because it does not give us a logical, rational view of God. Its insights cannot be reduced neatly to facts or ideas. Instead, the power of the Song lies in its ability to evoke a new way of relating to God. I hope and pray that my suggestions will help you hear God whispering words of love in your ear as you experience the depth of your longing for God.

Chapter

*Let
Him
Kiss
Me*

Song of Songs 1:1–8

Let Us Make Haste

The Song of Songs, which is Solomon's.
Let him kiss me with the kisses of his mouth!
For your love is better than wine,
    your anointing oils are fragrant,
your name is perfume poured out;
    therefore the maidens love you.
Draw me after you, let us make haste.
    The king has brought me into his chambers.
We will exult and rejoice in you;
    we will extol your love more than wine;
    rightly do they love you.

    (1:1–4)

The book begins with impatience.

At least in their beginnings, there is in all love relationships a sense of impatience. Early in the relationship, we are obsessed with our lover. Every thought is directed toward the object of our desire. We are consumed with a desire to be in the presence of our beloved. It seems that time without the beloved moves very, very slowly. So it is with the bride in the Song of Songs.

She begins with a desire for touch, particularly a desire for a kiss. "Let him kiss me with the kisses of his mouth!" (1:2a) Love is not content with remaining distant. It is not content with simply admiring. Love demands that solid touch of flesh on flesh. The desire, the longing for such a touch can be almost painful in its intensity.

It is characteristic of people in love that they cannot help but praise the one they love to those around them, and so the bride bursts into song in praise of the one she loves. She feels a need to communicate to those around her just how important that love is. Although words are always inadequate to describe love, lovers feel compelled to try, and this bride is no exception. She cries out that the groom's love is better than wine. His love is like fragrant anointing oils and poured-out perfume.

Although she cannot adequately describe the love of her beloved, the fact of their love is evident to those around her. Their love is not a private, secret thing. Instead it is a public matter, something that all can see. The quality of his love for the bride is such that all the maidens, not just the bride, come to love the groom. All are touched by the love flowing from the groom to the bride. All are included in some way.

The bride, having sung the praises of her lover, is impatient once more. Having been brought into the king's chambers, she waits eagerly for the coming of the king. Love is impatient, eager for its fulfillment. It will be satisfied with nothing less than all that it desires, and its desire can be satisfied only in the physical presence of the beloved.

So it is with our souls as well. We each have a deep longing for God. We may try to satisfy that longing with a whole host of other things. We may even mistake the longing for God for something else. We may think that what we most desire is food or alcohol, power or money—but we, like the bride, really desire the nearer presence of God. That is the real desire beneath all our longing, and the glory of romantic love is that it allows no other desires to get between the lovers. Bernard of Clairvaux celebrated just such a love. "Let those who have experienced it enjoy it; let those who have not burn with desire, not so much to know it as to experience it. It is not a noise made aloud, but the very music of the heart."[30]

Praying with the Song of Songs is one way to help us get in touch with our deep longing for God, symbolized by a kiss. It is one way to help us begin to fill our hearts and our minds with the sound of praise for our Beloved. It is one way to remind ourselves that we love and are loved intensely by God.

I Am Black and Beautiful

I am black and beautiful,
    O daughters of Jerusalem,
like the tents of Kedar,
    like the curtains of Solomon.
Do not gaze at me because I am dark,
    because the sun has gazed on me.
My mother's sons were angry with me;
    they made me keeper of the vineyards,
    but my own vineyard I have not kept!
      (1:5–6)

Aware that she is loved, the bride rejoices in her beauty. She sees herself not through her own eyes or the eyes of others, but through the eyes of the beloved.

She has not always been so cherished. She is aware that not everyone would rejoice in her sun-darkened skin, and she wants no stares because of it. She defies anyone to deny her dark beauty.

Her brothers have not cherished her. They have sent her to work in the vineyards, where the sun has gazed upon her. Because of their demands, she has not been able to properly tend her own vineyard. She possesses none of the beauty of one who spends much time making herself beautiful, but she is beautiful nonetheless. She is beautiful because she is loved, and she rejoices that the bridegroom sees in her that beauty. Because of the love of the bridegroom, she is beautiful, and she can proclaim it to all.

Too often we do not consider ourselves beautiful. Too often we are more aware of our flaws and weaknesses than our beauty. Too often we do not see ourselves as worthy of God's passionate love.

That is because we look at ourselves through the wrong set of eyes. We look at ourselves with the eyes of our culture, which tells us, for example, that we must be young and thin. We look at ourselves with the eyes of others, who may discount us because of our race or our disabilities. We look at ourselves with the eyes of those who may have criticized us when we were growing up, making us feel that we were never good enough. We look at ourselves with our own guilty eyes, knowing how far we are from what we would like to be.

The Song of Songs calls us to look at ourselves with another set of eyes. It calls us to look at ourselves through the eyes of the One who loves us—through God's eyes.

When we do, we are in for a surprise. For through the eyes of love, we are indeed beautiful, more beautiful than we could possibly imagine.

You Whom My Soul Loves

Tell me, you whom my soul loves,
    where you pasture your flock,
    where you make it lie down at noon;
for why should I be like one who is veiled
    beside the flocks of your companions?
If you do not know,
    O fairest among women,
follow the tracks of the flock,
    and pasture your kids
    beside the shepherds' tents.
      (1:7–8)

The bride, who has been waiting impatiently for the coming of the groom, wishes to wait no longer. She is no longer content to be a passive player in this romantic drama. If the groom will not come to her, she will go to him.

She hatches a daring plan. She will wait for him out in the pasture, far from the eyes of those who would expect her to behave with more propriety. At noon, when the sun is the highest and the heat of the day is most oppressive, both shepherds and flocks rest in the coolest spot they can find. The others will be napping, unlikely to notice her unauthorized presence. It is there that she plans to meet the one she loves.

There is only one problem with her plans. She does not know how to find her beloved. She is afraid that she will stumble into someone else's camp by mistake. She can imagine wandering aimlessly about the wrong camps, veiled to preserve propriety, and missing her beloved altogether. So she cries out to the beloved to help her in the plan. She needs him to tell her where to go.

The bridegroom answers his beloved, encouraging her to persevere in her search. He is a willing conspirator to her plans. He does not tell her exactly where to go, but he gives her a trail to follow. She will only need to follow the tracks of his flocks to find him. She can even bring her own kids, to give her a plausible excuse for being there. By the shepherd's tents she can pasture her kids, and presumably they can meet in the tents without fear of being seen.

As we begin our journey into deeper intimacy with God, it is not always clear to us where to go. We, like the bride, may be unsure how to find God, even if we long to do so. From a distance, many others may look like the One we seek, but will prove not to be the One we are looking for when we get close enough to see clearly. We can spend a lot of time wandering aimlessly.

Just as the bridegroom answered his beloved's call, however, when we call out to God, God will answer. God is a willing conspirator in our desire to come closer. Like the bride, we may not get a description of our final meeting place, but God will provide tracks that we may follow.

Our journey to God is much like tracking. Sometimes the tracks are clear and we can follow quickly. At other times they have become faded with time, wind, and rain, making the trail hard to discern. At those times we have to slow down, for fear of losing the trail completely. Occasionally we will be misled by other tracks, and wander off the original trail altogether. We may have to backtrack for quite a ways before we can once again pick it up.

God is, however, waiting for us at the shepherd's tents. God is waiting for us at the end of the trail. The tracks are there. Dare we follow them?

Journal Questions

1. The bride in the Song of Songs is impatiently waiting for her lover to appear. She wants his nearer presence, a presence that she symbolizes with a kiss. What do you most want from the Bridegroom? For what are you eagerly and impatiently waiting?

2. Over the course of our lives, we are repeatedly given messages about our physical appearance. What messages do you carry with you, and where do those messages come from? What do you think God would like to tell you about those messages, about your true self?

3. In your journal, draw a picture of the trail you have been following in your journey toward God. Label the times when the track has been easy to follow, when it has been difficult, and when you may have wandered off the path. How do you know when you are following the right path?

Suggestions for Prayer

1. Often a word or phrase is used to help people focus in silent prayer. Spend some time in silence, using the word Beloved to focus your prayer. If thoughts or feelings arise, note them to think about later. After your silence you might want to write in your journal about the experience. What new under-

standings of God did this way of addressing God open for you?

2. Ask God to help you discover that for which you are impatiently waiting. Spend some time in silence, allowing the answer to slowly surface. When it does, ask God to grant it to you.

3. Ask God to help you see yourself as God sees you. Spend some time being open to a new way of looking at yourself—through the eyes of love.

4. If you have not asked God to provide you a path to follow, ask as the bride does. Let God help you on this journey. Spend some time in silence listening for any clues that God may provide for the next stage of your journey.

Chapter

A Mare
Among
Pharaoh's
Chariots

Song of Songs 1:9–17

I Compare You, My Love

I compare you, my love,
    to a mare among Pharaoh's chariots.
Your cheeks are comely with ornaments,
    your neck with strings of jewels.
We will make you ornaments of gold,
    studded with silver.

    (1:9–11)

Now the groom begins his description of his beloved. It will not be the only time; there will be other descriptions later on. This is only a beginning, and yet I think that it is instructive to look at the first thing the groom says of his beloved.

He begins with a comparison. Although comparisons are by definition not exact descriptions, those in love find them invaluable for pointing toward the truth that cannot be expressed in a simple statement of facts. So the groom proclaims that his lover is like a mare among Pharaoh's chariots.

The image of the mare is an image of strength, speed, and beauty. Horses were prized in those times for all those qualities, and when the groom uses the analogy, it is meant to remind us of the grace and beauty of a mare.

However, the verse contains more than simply that image of beauty, for it is not just any mare that is mentioned, but a mare among Pharaoh's chariots. What does that additional phrase add to the picture of the bride?

Surely the choicest of horses would be found in Pharaoh's stable. Possibly it adds an additional element of beauty, speed, and grace. It could simply be a way of indicating that the bride is not only as beautiful as a mare, but as beautiful as the most beautiful of mares.

There is a problem, however, with that image. Mares were never found among Pharaoh's chariots. Only stallions were used to pull the great war machines.

It is possible that the groom was simply unaware that mares were never used in battle. Lovers, in the imagination of their hearts, are not limited to mere pictures of reality. Having seen magnificent horses pulling the chariots, he may simply, in his mind's eye, have placed a mare among them.

According to Marcia Falk, another, more interesting possibility exists. The Pharaoh's enemies would "set mares loose in war to drive the pharaoh's stallions wild, and this is the crux of the metaphor. The woman is not simply a beautiful creature; she is as alluring as 'a mare among stallions.' "[31] Falk's translation of verse 9 adds a different dimension to the meaning. "Like a mare among stallions, You lure, I am held."[32]

Could it be that the groom is saying that the bride has as much power over him as a mare has over a stallion? As the war stallions could not resist the mares, neither can the groom resist the charms of his beloved. As the stallions were driven wild by the mares, so the groom is driven wild by the bride.

We have all seen people in love (or been in love ourselves) and experienced the power of that attraction. Lovers will do anything necessary to be together. Pulling them apart has painful and sometimes tragic results.

We can imagine that being the case with human lovers. But can we imagine that we might have that kind of power over God? Can we imagine that God might desire us so much that we would be as alluring as a mare among stallions? Can we imagine that God would allow such a situation to take place? It is a startling idea!

It certainly does not fit with the idea of an impassive God, unmoved by human emotions. In fact, the Bible paints a picture of a passionate God, a God who can be mightily moved by humans. The Bible reminds us that God loves us fiercely and passionately.

In loving us, God has given us a certain power over God. What we do and who we are matter to God. We do not have the power to coerce God, anymore than that kind of power is a part of healthy human love. We do not have the power to bend God to our will. That is not the power of love.

The power of love is a power of attraction, of allure, of irresistibility. The power of love draws the lovers ever closer to each other. The power of love is not meant to exercise control but to join the two into one.

We are irresistible to God, and if we let ourselves, we will be irresistibly drawn to God as well. That is the power of love.

My Beloved Is to Me . . .

While the king was on his couch,
    my nard gave forth its fragrance.
My beloved is to me a bag of myrrh
    that lies between my breasts.
My beloved is to me a cluster of henna blossoms
    in the vineyards of En-gedi.
    (1:12–14)

The praises go back and forth. Now it is the bride's turn to talk of her beloved, to describe him, or rather his effect on her. The praise of the groom for the bride evokes praise for the groom in turn.

The images that the bride uses evoke the sense of smell. She speaks first of the smell of her nard, which reached the king on his couch. Lovers enjoy any reminder of their beloved; even smells associated with them are hallowed by association.

Having turned her attention to smell, she tries to capture something of her beloved in images of scent. He is like a bag of myrrh and a cluster of henna blossoms, powerfully giving forth their fragrance and sweetening the air. Although she smells of nard from her cosmetics, he is also sweet-smelling in his very essence.

Like the image of the mare, these are not simple images. The bride speaks not just of myrrh, but of a bag of myrrh between her breasts. She speaks not just of henna blossoms, but of henna blossoms in the vineyards of En-gedi. She speaks of place as well as object.

The bride wishes that her beloved were lying in her arms. She wishes to hold him as close to her heart as a bag of myrrh between her breasts. Then their separation would be over. Then would they be as one.

According to Ann Koepke, in *Herbs and Flowers in the Bible*,[33] myrrh has no discernible odor unless it is either damp or warm. Lying close to her chest will cause it to release its aroma, as holding her lover closer to her chest will heighten the scent of their love.

The bride also compares her beloved to henna blossoms in the vineyards of En-gedi. En-gedi is a place of springs, of green and verdant growth. The vineyards of En-gedi would be bursting with juice and life. They would be fruitful, as fruitful as the love of the bride and her beloved.

We, like the bride, are to dream of the time when God will seem as close to us as a bag of myrrh lying against our chest. We are called to imagine God being as real as the smell of myrrh that drifts up from up there. We, like the bride, are to savor the scent of God.

We are also invited to imagine a time when our love, the love that we share with God, is bursting with life in the same way as well-watered vineyards. We are to taste and see that our Lover is God, and that our love is indeed beautiful.

Our Couch Is Green

Ah, you are beautiful, my love;
  ah, you are beautiful;
  your eyes are doves.

Ah, you are beautiful, my beloved,
    truly lovely.
Our couch is green;
    the beams of our house are cedar,
    our rafters are pine.
        (1:15–17)

Although love can be shared and celebrated anywhere, there is something special about the outdoors. Often lovers will find a way to be together, not in the confines of a house, but in the openness of creation. It is almost as if their love cannot be constrained by walls. Or perhaps they simply want to be out of the sight of others to celebrate their love in privacy.

After losing himself again in her beauty, the groom describes the place of their meeting, the place where they will share their love. It is not a fancy house with a couch of gold. It is not a bed with the finest linens. Overcome with love, they have no need for all the trappings.

They find a suitable place to share their love. Their couch is made of grass and leaves. The walls of their bower are cedar trees. Overhead, pine trees shelter them from the sun. In their bower, they have no need of anything, and they can turn their full attention to each other.

Sometimes a special place can help us be more aware of God, but God has no need of fancy houses. Sometimes God will appear in the most unexpected places. For lovers, wherever the beloved is to be found is the most important place in the world.

Journal Questions

1. What have you been doing to try to entice God to notice you? How does it make you feel to imagine that you might be as alluring to God as a mare is among the pharaoh's war stallions?

2. If you wanted to express your sense of God in a smell, which smell would it be? Would it be sweet, spicy, strong?

3. Where have you encountered God? What particular places have you found that make it easier to be in the presence of God?

Suggestions for Prayer

1. If you have been trying a particular type of prayer, put it aside for a little while. Trust that you are alluring to God as you are, and that if you remain still and quiet, God will be drawn to you. You need not try to do anything. Simply be still in the presence of God.

2. Experiment with scent in your prayers. During prayer, try using a scented candle or incense to engage your sense of smell.

3. Experiment with prayer in different places. If you have a place that has been important in your relationship with God, you might want to return there. You might also want to set aside a particular place for meeting with God. A picture, a candle, a Bible, or other items can mark it as special.

4. Take a walk in the woods and imagine that you are walking with your Lover. Ask God to join you on this walk, and enjoy the beauty of creation with the One you love.

Chapter

5

His Intention Toward Me Was Love

Song of Songs 2:1–7

Sweet to My Taste

I am a rose of Sharon,
> a lily of the valleys.
As a lily among brambles,
> so is my love among maidens.
As an apple tree among the trees of the wood,
> so is my beloved among young men.
With great delight I sat in his shadow,
> and his fruit was sweet to my taste.

>> *(2:1–3)*

Again the bride, confident of the groom's love, exults in her own beauty. She compares herself to the flowers growing wild and beautiful around her. Like the lily of the valley, a spring plant, her love and her beauty are both in their springtime.

Her boast is affirmed and even strengthened by the groom. Not only is she a lily, but she is like a lily surrounded by brambles, all the more precious and surprising in its beauty for being found in the midst of them. The contrast sharpens that sense of beauty and makes all else look like weeds.

In response to the groom's affirmation of her beauty, the bride again returns to one of her favorite themes: the wonder of her beloved. If she is the lily among the brambles, he is an apple tree among the trees of the forest. Both are remarkable, for they are incongruous in their settings.

The groom stands out in this section, not so much for his beauty (although the bride is not shy about praising his beauty elsewhere), but for his fruit. He is an apple tree bursting with fruit. Among men, his is fruit beyond compare, and the fruit she desires is his love. Eugene Peterson translates verse 3, "All I want is to sit in his shade, to taste and savor his delicious love."[34]

She rejoices to be close to her lover and to rest in his shadow. His presence covers her and provides a place of comfort and refreshment. His glances, his words, his kisses, his touch are like the sweetest fruit. She eats and is delighted.

It is in the nature of lovers to rejoice in each other and to try to outdo each other with praises of the other. In this section we have an example of their direct dialogue with each other. These are not hymns to impress an audience, but short pieces meant to convey the depth of their love for each other. There is almost a sense of being drunk on each other.

Like the lovers, we are meant to be drunk with our love for God. To be in the presence of God, to feel and hear of God's love for us, is meant to draw out a response in us. Love that provokes no response in the one who is loved is stunted. Its full flowering comes when the energy and love of two swell into one joyous refrain of adoration.

Do Not Stir Up or Awaken Love

He brought me to the banqueting house,
    and his intention toward me was love.
Sustain me with raisins,
    refresh me with apples;
    for I am faint with love.
O that his left hand were under my head,
    and that his right hand embraced me!
I adjure you, O daughters of Jerusalem,
    by the gazelles or the wild does:
do not stir up or awaken love
    until it is ready!
      (2:4–7)

Memories play an important part in the development of love. When the lovers cannot be together, the memory of times when they shared love can sustain them until their next meeting. The bride remembers their time together. She remembers when the groom brought her to a banqueting house. She remembers a time when they shared food together, often a powerful way of forging connections of love.

It is not, however, the food that is the most important part of the memory. She does not talk about what they ate when they were together. She may not even remember the menu for that night. What she remembers is the time spent together, time that forges the bonds of love ever more deeply. The groom's intention was not simply to satisfy their hunger for food, but to satisfy their hunger for love and for each other. His intention, according to the bride, was love.

Remembering this meal, made marvelous by the company, she feels faint in his absence. Not having the food of his presence, she turns to other food for sustenance. She calls on her attendants to bring her food, so that it may revive her. That food, however, can never fully sustain her, for she is not afflicted with a normal hunger. Her hunger is for the beloved. She is faint with love, or alternately she is in the fever of love.[35]

She knows what she needs to combat this sickness. She knows what would fully revive her. It is her beloved's presence. She craves his touch. She wants to be fully embraced by him so that they may be as close as possible. That is the only thing that would cure her illness.

She addresses her attendants with a caution. Love is a powerful force, and not to be trifled with. It is not something to take lightly. It can be dangerous. It is like a bed of coals, ready to be stirred into a blazing flame. She knows, for she is on fire with her love for the groom.

She does not want, however, to be saved from that fire. Instead, she wants to be consumed by it. Marcia Falk's translation brings out that aspect. This love is explosive in its power and all consuming.

> O women of the city,
> Swear by the wild field doe
> Not to wake or rouse us
> Till we fulfill our love.[36]

The bride is looking anxiously toward the fulfillment of her love. She is looking forward to the time when at last their love can be consummated, and she wants nothing to interfere with that for which she has eagerly waited. She makes her maidens swear to give them the space and time they need to fulfill the promise of their love.

Our memories of God are one of the things that keep our love alive as well. Those times of particular closeness strengthen and sustain us during the times when we may feel that God is far away. Those special times may also awaken in us a desire to move closer to God. We may experience a desire to be held close in God's loving arms.

We are hungry as well. Like the bride, we need nourishment. In the absence of the groom, we may rely on other things to satisfy our hunger, but they are only temporary measures. Since we are faint with love, only sharing our love with God will really satisfy our deep longing.

It can be difficult, as the bride knows, to find time to be alone with God. We may have trouble finding the time and space our love needs to grow and become fulfilled. Our love grows in those times when we can be alone with God, fully focused on God and the love we share.

Journal Questions

1. The bride imagines her lover as an apple tree. Think about your experience of God. What images come to mind for you? Write, draw, or use some other type of artistic medium to craft those images. What qualities do those images call to mind?

2. Remember a time when you felt close to God. Recall it as deeply as you can, and write down what you remember. Where were you? What made it special? Can you remember any sights, sounds, smells, or touches associated with that time?

3. What gets in the way of spending time alone with God? What would you need to do to claim that time as the bride does? Are there people (e.g., family) you need to ask not to disturb you?

Suggestions for Prayer

1. Imagine yourself in a room with God. What would you say about yourself? What would God answer in turn? What would you say about your Lover? Engage your Lover in conversation, and listen for God's response to you.

2. Picture yourself sitting in the shadow of God's tree. Rest in that place, allowing God to nurture your soul by presence and by silence.

3. Ask God to help you feel your growing desire for intimacy with God. Spend some time in silence, and allow your feelings of love to rise closer to the surface.

Chapter

Come Away

Song of Songs 2:8–17

The Voice of My Beloved

The voice of my beloved!
   Look, he comes,
leaping upon the mountains,
   bounding over the hills.
My beloved is like a gazelle
   or a young stag.
Look, there he stands
   behind our wall,
gazing in at the windows,
   looking through the lattice.

(2:8–9)

The joy and excitement of the bride can scarcely be contained. The bridegroom's voice is enough to send her into a rapture. It means that he has finally come.

In her joy she bursts out in a song of praise of her beloved. She compares him to a graceful animal leaping on the mountains and bounding over the hills. In his grace, beauty, and power, he reminds her of a gazelle or a young stag. In motion he is glorious to watch.

Peeking out from behind the wall, she rejoices in his presence. Finally he has come, and not only has he come, he is also searching for her. She sees him looking in the windows, trying to catch a glimpse of her in the house. He looks through the lattice, trying to see the bride. She is being sought, actively!

So God is also seeking us. We have many ways of hiding from God, but God will keep looking until we have been discovered. In the end we will not be able to hide from God. We will be found.

Like the bride, we want to catch sight of God bounding over

the hills toward us. We want to be sought. Deep down inside us, we want to be found.

Like the bride, our heart gives a leap of joy at the sound of the Groom's voice. At last, the Groom is coming! At last our Beloved has come for us. At last, the time of our meeting is here. Our waiting has come to an end.

Arise, My Love

My beloved speaks and says to me:
"Arise, my love, my fair one,
    and come away;
for now the winter is past,
    the rain is over and gone.
The flowers appear on the earth;
    the time of singing has come,
and the voice of the turtledove
    is heard in our land.
The fig tree puts forth its figs,
    and the vines are in blossom;
    they give forth fragrance.
Arise, my love, my fair one,
    and come away.
Oh my dove, in the clefts of the rock,
    in the covert of the cliff,
let me see your face,
    let me hear your voice;
for your voice is sweet,
    and your face is lovely."
    (2:10–14)

With the coming of the bridegroom, winter is over. All around, new life is bursting forth. The rainy season has ended, and the plants and animals respond to this change. Flowers bloom, vines blossom, and figs appear on the trees. Turtledoves sing their songs. All creation is affected. Spring arrives.[37]

Love also brings forth its own springtime. Whatever the weather may be, when love blossoms, all creation is affected. The world seems to be filled with enchantment and life. As the bride and groom come together again, spring comes for them as well.

Of all the beauty in creation, however, nothing is more beautiful to the groom than the bride. He longs to see her face, a face that reminds him of a dove. Like a dove in the cleft of the rock, her face is still hidden from him behind the wall, and he is anxious to see her once again. He cannot find her. Perhaps she is playfully hiding from her lover![38]

He is anxious to hear her voice as well. It is sweet to his ears, as his voice was to the bride. To see her, to hear her voice, is to be in her presence once again.

Yet he wants more than to simply see and hear her; he wants to be able to take her away to a place that is less public, a place for only the two of them, a place where they can focus only on each other. He urges her repeatedly to come away. "Arise, my love, my fair one, and come away," he entreats her.

When we are in God's presence, there is life and love, and in the presence of love, it is always springtime. When we are in God's presence, the world is enchanted. When we are in God's presence, all creation is affected. In the presence of our Lover, in the presence of God, spring bursts forth all around us.

Like the lover in this passage, God is coming to meet us. Like him, God is singing our praises. God invites us to come away, for God wants to see our face and hear our voice. Of course, we are always in God's sight, and God can always hear our voice. But God wants more than to simply catch a glimpse of us as we hurry on to other things, more than to simply eavesdrop on our conversations with others. Like the lover in the Song, God wants us for God's self. God wants us to come away so that we can focus only on each other.

Arise, my love, my fair one, and come away. God is calling.

Catch Us the Foxes

"Catch us the foxes,
    the little foxes,
that ruin the vineyards—
    for our vineyards are in blossom."
    (2:15)

It is a curious interlude. Who or what are the foxes in this text? Foxes were considered to be pests in ancient texts, particularly in vineyards.[39] In fables, too, foxes were often portrayed as ravaging vineyards.[40] Presumably, then, the speaker is expressing concern that their vineyard might be destroyed by someone or something.

It is actually difficult to be sure who is speaking in this passage. Nevertheless, blossoming vineyards have been used so often in the book for the love that is shared between the bride and groom that we can assume the speaker is one of the lovers.

There is, then, a concern that something or someone will spoil the love that is blossoming between them. Care needs to be taken to protect this love, which is special and important, from all that might damage or ruin it.

Things can interfere in the blossoming of our vineyards with God. We can be distracted by the cares of life. We can be dissuaded by others from pursuing the relationship. We can be tempted by other loves. Like the lovers, we need to catch the foxes before they ruin what is infinitely precious to us and to God.

My Beloved Is Mine

My beloved is mine and I am his;
    he pastures his flock among the lilies.
Until the day breathes
    and the shadows flee,
turn, my beloved, be like a gazelle
    or a young stag on the cleft mountains.
    (2:16–17)

The song returns to the bride. In strong language, she claims the groom for her own and gives herself to him just as irrevocably. Nothing will be allowed to separate them, for they belong to each other.

He pastures his flocks among the lilies. That might be a puzzling image, but in verse 1, the bride claims to be a lily of the valleys, and in the following verse, the groom affirms that the bride is a lily among the brambles. These are no ordinary lilies, but the bride's lilies among which he pastures his flock!

It is further affirmed that this pasturing will continue until the day breathes and the shadows flee. In other words, whatever happens will happen until morning comes. It will happen all through the night![41]

The bride, not satisfied simply to meet her lover in the day, in the company of others, longs to spend a whole night with him. She longs to have their love consummated. They belong together, and it is right and fitting that he pastures his flocks among her lilies. Knowing that others will not agree, she urges him, after their night together, to turn like a gazelle or a young stag on the cleft mountains and disappear in the morning.

We can also claim, along with the bride, that our Beloved is ours and we are our Beloved's. We belong completely to God. God belongs to us as well, for God has given God's self to us. Like the bride and the groom, we belong together.

We can also invite and long for the day when that love will be consummated, when God will pasture God's flock among our lilies. In that day we, too, will be fruitful, filled with the life and love and joy that only God can bring to us. Not everyone will understand the love we share with God, but in the end that does not matter. All that matters is that we are together forever.

Journal Questions

1. What ways do you have of hiding from God? What excuses do you find to avoid time with your Beloved?

2. Imagine what the springtime of your relationship with God would look like. Use words or some other artistic medium to capture the image. Craft a place for just you and your Lover.

3. What are the foxes that might ruin the blossoms in your vineyard with God? How can you prevent them from damaging that love?

4. In the last section, the images become more obviously sexual. Spend some time considering how you feel about the use of sexual imagery in relationship to God. What were you taught about sexuality by your family or in your religious tradition? How has that affected the ways in which you relate to God? How has that influenced the ways in which you view your own sexuality?

Suggestions for Prayer

1. Imagine God looking for you. Where would God have to look to find you?

2. Spend some time in silence, using the phrase "Come away with me" to center yourself. Do you hear God calling to you to come away?

3. Distractions are common in times of silence. Thoughts and words can overrun our minds, like the foxes overrun the vineyard. Ask God to help you catch the foxes so that you can enjoy the blossoming vineyard.

4. Often, in prayer, we terminate our time with God prematurely. Try to lengthen the time that you spend in silent prayer with God. If you cannot pray until the day breathes and the shadows flee (which few will be able to do), try to lengthen it by a short amount of time (5 or 10 minutes). This will help you develop the capacity to spend longer times with God.

Chapter

I Sought Him Whom My Soul Loves

Song of Songs 3:1–5

I Called Him, But He Gave No Answer

Upon my bed at night
  I sought him whom my soul loves;
I sought him, but found him not;
  I called him, but he gave no answer.
"I will rise now and go about the city,
  in the streets and in the squares;
I will seek him whom my soul loves."
  I sought him, but found him not.

  (3:1–2)

In the dark of night, the bride turns over in her bed, expecting her lover to be beside her. Perhaps he has been there earlier. Or perhaps she has had a dream in which they were together. Sleepily she gropes around in the bed, but does not find him.

She calls out, hoping that he is within range of her voice. She waits for a reply, but there is no answering voice. As incomprehensible as it seems to her, he is gone, and she is alone.

That state is intolerable for one who is in love. She needs to be with her lover. She needs to find him. She cannot simply lie in bed hoping that he will return. She decides, almost without thought, to go and look for him.

Although it is nighttime, she decides to search the streets and the squares. It is dark, but she fears loneliness more. It could be dangerous, but facing danger is better than facing the night without her beloved. She is frantic to find him.

There are times in our life of prayer when we turn to God, and it seems as if we are alone. There are times when we cannot find God in our accustomed places. And there are times when we cry out, and we hear no answering response. We may seek and yet not find the one whom we seek.

Such a time was known by the mystics as a dark night. It echoes well the darkness that surrounds the bride as she searches for her beloved. It can be a time of fear, of danger, of stumbling in the dark. Like the bride, however, we may need to be willing to enter that darkness to find the one we love.

Would Not Let Him Go

The sentinels found me,
    as they went about in the city.
"Have you seen him whom my soul loves?"
Scarcely had I passed them,
    when I found him whom my soul loves.
I held him, and would not let him go
    until I brought him into my mother's house,
      and into the chamber of her that conceived me.
I adjure you, O daughters of Jerusalem,
    by the gazelles or the wild does:
do not stir up or awaken love
    until it is ready!"
      (3:3–5)

Fleeing into the night, the bride is single-mindedly focused on her quest to find the one whom her soul loves. Nothing can dissuade her. Nothing can discourage her. She will not stop until she finds him and they are together once again.

Encountering the sentinels on their rounds, she enlists them in her frantic search. It is not clear what their response was; either they were of no help or they refused to help. Her description of the groom as the one whom her soul loves is scarcely helpful. It might indeed be his most important characteristic, but it scarcely helps the sentinels pick him out of a group of men.

In spite of her lack of success, the bride continues her search. She leaves the sentinels behind and goes further on. Finally her search is rewarded. She finds the one whom her soul loves, and she can scarcely contain her joy.

She holds onto him, refusing to let him go. She will not let him slip from her side again; they will be together. She leads or perhaps even drags him to her mother's house. We have no idea what the groom thinks of this behavior. All we know is that she is indeed successful in her quest.

She brings him not only into her mother's house but also into her mother's bedchamber, into the place where she herself had been conceived. There is little doubt of her intentions toward the beloved. The suggestions are all there. In the place where her parents' love was consummated, she wishes to consummate her own love.

The bride then returns to her earlier admonition to the daughters of Jerusalem (found also in 2:7). The loss of the bridegroom, her frantic search, and the relief when he has been found have all aroused her. She is well aware of the power that has been awakened in her, a force that will not be denied. She warns them not to toy with it, for love has the power to consume those who fall into its power.

Marcia Falk's translation offers a different reading (see Suggestions for Prayer, at the end of this chapter). The bride also warns the women not to disturb her and the groom. They will retreat from public view, and do not wish to be disturbed until they have fulfilled their love.

What do we do when we awaken and realize that we cannot feel God's presence with us? What do we do in the dark of the night when we are alone? What do we do when God has seemingly slipped away?

If God is really the most important thing in the world to us, as the groom is to the bride, we will be willing to put aside everything else to search. If God is the one whom our soul loves, then we will not be deterred by darkness or danger. If God is that important to us, we will be willing to race through the darkness, searching desperately for some sign of God.

True love is not complacent. True love is not willing to wait passively, on the off chance that the object of the love will return. True love is willing to risk all for the sake of the beloved.

It can, at times, be dark. Without the light of God's presence beside us, the search can seem very dangerous. We may decide that it is prudent to wait for morning, but if our sun has vanished, morning will not come simply by waiting.

We are called to search for our Lover in times of darkness. Like the bride, we are to question all those we meet, hoping for some clue as to where our Beloved may have gone. We may have to search high and low, but God is in that darkness. If we are willing to enter the darkness, we will find all that we desire within.

We will be allowed to drag God home with us, at least for a while. God is willing to be brought into that place of extreme intimacy. The Groom, as much as the bride, yearns to fulfill their love.

Do not give up. Search all the dark streets and squares. Your Lover is waiting to be found!

Journal Questions

1. Recall a time when God seemed absent to you. How would you describe your dark night(s)? Of what were you afraid?

2. How do you respond in those times when God seems absent?

3. As you have searched for God, whom have you questioned along the way? In what ways have they been helpful or unhelpful in the search?

4. When you find God, how do you respond? In what ways is your response similar to or different from the bride's?

5. How great is your desire for God right now? Has your level of desire changed as you have been praying the Song of Songs?

Suggestions for Prayer

1. Picture yourself lying or sitting in an elaborate chamber. Turn to the side and check to see if God is there with you.

   a. If you feel God next to you, spend time in God's presence, enjoying time together as lovers do. At the end of your prayer time, give thanks for what you have experienced.

   b. If you do not feel God next to you, call out and see if your Lover is within earshot. If you hear an answer, spend some time in God's presence.

   c. If there is no answer, picture what you will do in your Beloved's absence. How is love calling you to respond?

2. Fear often keeps us from drawing closer to God. At the beginning of your prayer time, ask God to help you to be aware of your fears. In the silence, be open to whatever arises. If you become aware of fears as you pray, end your prayer time by asking God to help you draw closer in spite of your fears.

3. Use Marcia Falk's version of chapter 3, verse 5 to center your prayers:

   > O women of the city,
   >> Swear by the wild field doe
   >> Not to wake or rouse us
   >> Till we fulfill our love.[42]

Allow yourself simply to be with God in the silence, trusting that whatever you need to grow in your love of God will be given to you.

Chapter

8

*Daughters
of
Jerusalem,
Come Out*

Song of Songs 3:6–11

What Is That Coming?

What is that coming up from the wilderness,
   like a column of smoke,
perfumed with myrrh and frankincense,
   with all the fragrant powders of the merchant?
Look, it is the litter of Solomon!
Around it are sixty mighty men
   of the mighty men of Israel,
all equipped with swords
   and expert in war,
each with his sword at his thigh
   because of alarms by night.

    (3:6–8)

Eagerly the bride waits. Eagerly she searches for signs that her beloved is coming.

Finally she sees a sign. Someone is coming—a large group of people, raising dust as they advance. It must be the beloved in his wedding train. The smoke of their passage becomes sweet to her because of what it portends. It is as if it were perfumed with the fragrant powders of the merchant—scented with the costly smells of myrrh and frankincense.

Still the bride strains eagerly to catch the first glimpse of her beloved. As the procession draws closer, she begins to make out details. Although she has yet to catch a glimpse of her beloved, all the signs point to his presence. The first thing she sees is a litter on which someone of great importance is being carried. It must be the bridegroom, being carried to his wedding.

The litter is surrounded by the flower of manhood—a mighty group of men—cutting off the groom from her sight. The men are carrying swords, advertising their military prowess. It is indeed a marvelous and magnificent procession. No one would dare to attack it, no matter where it goes.

Like the bride, we are called to watch and wait for the One we love. We do not know how long it will be before we get the first intimations that God is coming to meet us. Like the bride, we are to strain eagerly to find those signs and to rejoice in the signs of God's coming.

Even when we get signs of God's presence, we may not get a direct glimpse of God. We may, like the bride at first, see only the signs that the procession stirs up, like the sighting of dust in the desert. We may see only the people surrounding the litter, but not God in the midst of the crowd.

Even when the first signs come, we may still have to watch and wait, hoping for a glimpse of the One we love.

Inlaid with Love

> King Solomon made himself a palanquin
>   from the wood of Lebanon.
> He made its posts of silver,
>   its back of gold, its seat of purple;
> its interior was inlaid with love.
>   (3:9–10a)

A palanquin is a covered litter. In such a thing, the groom would still be hidden from the sight of the eagerly waiting bride. She cannot yet see him, or her descriptions would not be of the palanquin but of him. After all, it is he for whom she waits, not his mode of transport, no matter how magnificent.

Unable to see him, however, she must content herself with admiring the beauty of the palanquin, rather than the beauty of her lover. The litter is made of all the finest materials, a fitting tribute for her beloved. Wood from Lebanon, the finest wood available, was used to make it, and it is adorned with silver and gold. The seat is of costly royal purple. In the beauty and magnificence of its creation, the bride sees the even greater beauty of her lover reflected.

Most important to the bride, however, is that the interior of the palanquin is inlaid with love. The groom, reclining inside, is surrounded by love. He is surrounded by the bride's love for him and his love for her. That love shines even brighter than the silver posts and the gold back.

God has no palanquin, but like the bride, we sometimes receive glimpses of God's beauty in the things God has created. Sunsets and waterfalls, woods and streams, animals and birds, flowers and trees all reflect the glory of God in the same way the wood from Lebanon, silver, gold, and purple reflect the glory of the groom to the bride.

Nature can be like God's palanquin. In nature we may not be confronted with God face to face, but in nature's glory, the glory of God is reflected. We can rejoice in that beauty, knowing that it is indeed a reflection of the beauty of our Beloved.

Most of all, we can rejoice that the beauty of nature is an expression of God's love for us and for all creation. When we look around, we see signs of God's loving care again and again. The beauty and complexity of nature, the way all its parts fit so carefully together, are evidence of a master creator who works hard to ensure that all is inlaid with love.

On the Day of His Wedding

> Daughters of Jerusalem,
> come out.
> Look, O daughters of Zion,
> at King Solomon,
> at the crown with which his mother crowned him
> on the day of his wedding,
> on the day of the gladness of his heart.

(3:10b–11)

The bride rejoices; the long-awaited day has come at last. The groom, decked out in his wedding finery, has arrived. She rejoices in his presence, and she invites others to join in the celebration—for the coming together of the bride and the groom is a cause of great celebration. Love, at some point, needs to declare itself to the world. Love, at some point, needs to show the world what can no longer be contained.

Much of our life with God is private; much is shared only between God and ourselves. Love, however, cannot remain secret forever. Love longs to be proclaimed from the housetops. Love desires public affirmation. That is why lovers marry. That is why we are also called to make public our commitment to and love of God.

Journal Questions

1. Do you see signs of God's coming? If so, what are they? If not, what could you imagine might be a sign of God coming to you?

2. Do certain places or objects remind you of God? How does God's beauty shine through the things around you?

3. In what ways do you make public your love of God? How do you celebrate with others?

Suggestions for Prayer

1. Spend some time in silence waiting for God to come to you. Look for any signs of God's impending arrival.

2. Be aware of the things around you. As you are struck with beauty, pause and let the beauty of the object speak to you of the beauty of the Creator.

3. Pick a corner in your home for prayer. Spend some time deciding how to make a beautiful "palanquin." Use pictures, items from nature, or other works of art to beautify your meeting place with God. Make sure it is inlaid with love.

4. If you are not regularly attending worship, find a place where you can publicly affirm your love for God and God's love for you. If you are already a part of a community, rejoice with the daughters of Jerusalem.

Chapter

You Are Altogether Beautiful

Song of Songs 4:1–8

Your Eyes Are Doves

How beautiful you are, my love,
>how very beautiful!
Your eyes are doves
>behind your veil.
Your hair is like a flock of goats,
>moving down the slopes of Gilead.
Your teeth are like a flock of shorn ewes
>that have come up from the washing,
all of which bear twins,
>and not one among them is bereaved.
Your lips are like a crimson thread,
>and your mouth is lovely.
Your cheeks are like halves of a pomegranate
>behind your veil.
Your neck is like the tower of David,
>built in courses;
on it hang a thousand bucklers,
>all of them shields of warriors.
Your two breasts are like two fawns,
>twins of a gazelle,
>that feed among the lilies.
>>*(4:1–5)*

Gazing at his beloved, the groom bursts into a song of praise. He feels that he must sing of her beauty and her grace. It is her presence that draws out that praise. Although no image can equal the sight of his beloved, lovers feel compelled to try to describe each other, and the groom brings forth the most wonderful images that he knows.

"How beautiful you are," he exclaims. "How very beautiful!"

Heartfelt as they are, those words do not begin to describe her beauty. He wants to capture that beauty, to remember it when they are apart, to be able to sing it to others, and so he begins to describe her lovingly, starting from the top of her head. "She is *his* world and in her he sees every sight which has ever stirred in him the emotions of awe, wonder and worship."[43]

Her eyes are like doves behind her veil. Doves seem to be an image that comes to mind frequently for the groom when speaking of his beloved. In chapter 1, he also describes the bride's eyes like doves. In chapter 2, as she is playing hide and seek with him behind the wall, he describes her as a dove hidden in the cliff. The soft gentle dove is a reminder to him of the soft eyes of the one he loves.

Her hair, as it cascades down her shoulders, reminds him of the movement and grace of a flock of goats running down a hillside. The sun glints off the waves of her hair in the same way that the sun catches the coats of the goats. It is a scene full of movement and life, and the swirl of her hair around her is an affirmation of beauty and life.

Next he moves on to her teeth. They are shining white, like a flock of ewes that has just been shorn and bathed. They glisten in the light. No teeth are missing to mar her beauty. Instead each one is precisely paired, like twin lambs.

He next moves on to describe her mouth. It is as bright and lovely a red as a crimson thread, valued for the brilliance of its color. The colors of the weavers cannot make anything more lovely than her lips and mouth.

Her cheeks, curving behind her veil, are also elements that excite praise in the groom. They remind him of the graceful curve of the pomegranate fruit, a symbol of fertility.[44] Their blush is like the red color of the fruit.

Her neck is long and white. In its beauty, her neck reminds him of the tower of David in all its glory. As the tower was decorated with bucklers and shields, adding to its glory, so, too, the neck of the bride is adorned. It is adorned with necklaces and other jewelry, and is as magnificent in its way as David's tower is with its complement of war paraphernalia. (It is, however, a forbidding image, possibly reflecting the groom's view that she is inaccessible to him.)[45]

The bride earlier had compared the groom to a gazelle. Now the groom uses the gazelle as an image of the bride. Instead of a full-grown gazelle, full of strength and power, however, it is the fawns of the gazelle that remind him of his beloved. Their shy beauty and grace seem fitting reminders of the beauty of her breasts. They, too, are twins, paired and perfectly matched. The twins feed among the lilies, earlier a symbol of their love.

All this description could be quite embarrassing if it were your body that was being described. It may have been appropriate that the cheeks of the bride were compared with a red pomegranate. She was probably blushing!

As embarrassing as it may seem, however, love thrives on such descriptions. Rare is the lover who does not offer his or her praise, no matter how haltingly. Rare is the lover who does not try to find some way of describing the beloved, even while lamenting the inadequacy of words and images.

In such talk, the ones being described come to see themselves in a new light. They do not see themselves reflected through the messages of society or the harshness of a mirror. Instead they see themselves through the eyes of love. Through love they are able to see new things about themselves. In that reflection they are able to see themselves as beautiful.

We may not use the same images for beauty that the groom did in the Song of Songs; times and images change. Few of us have seen goats cascading down the slopes of Gilead. Images change, as times and cultures change, but the beauty remains. God is singing our praises just as fervently as the groom sings the praises of the bride.

It may be hard for us to believe, but we are as beautiful to God as the bride is to the bridegroom. We have been wonderfully and marvelously made. It does not matter what we have been told by our society; we are beautiful. It does not matter what we see when we look in the mirror; we are beautiful. It does not matter what we think about ourselves; we are beautiful. We are beautiful when seen through the eyes of our Lover. Listen, God is singing to you!

There Is No Flaw in You

> Until the day breathes
>   and the shadows flee,
> I will hasten to the mountain of myrrh
>   and the hill of frankincense.
> You are altogether beautiful, my love;
>   there is no flaw in you.
>   (4:6–7)

Again, the groom speaks of spending time with his beloved. He wants to be with her until the day breathes and the shadows flee. As in chapter 2, he wants to stay with her through the night.

Having just extolled her beauty with a whole set of images, he continues in the same way. It is not some known mountain of myrrh that he wants to visit. The myrrh plant is a small thorny tree, and a mountain of myrrh would hardly be an image of beauty. It is not some remembered hill of frankincense that draws his attention. As before, myrrh and frankincense, prized and highly valued for their odor, are images of the love that the bride and groom share.

The mountain of myrrh to which he plans to hasten is the mountain of myrrh that is a part of his beloved's body. The hill of frankincense is the one found on her. Like the bride, he is eager to spend a night together so that they can explore and consummate their love. Their love is like the costly odor of those valuable spices. His beloved's body can be described only with such images.

Having with delicacy described the remainder of her body, he now sums it all up. She is altogether beautiful. The parts, each beautiful in its own right, are even more beautiful when combined in the body of his bride. The whole effect is magnificent. Indeed, looking at her, he declares that she is flawless, perfect.

God is eagerly waiting to spend the night with us as well. God longs for our union with every bit as much eagerness as the groom longs for the bride. The love that we are to share is, to God, like the perfume of the most costly spices.

That may be hard for us to believe. It may be hard to think that God prizes us that highly. We may think that that happens only with certain special people.

In the eyes of love, however, the lover is always special. God loves us, and loves us deeply—far more deeply than a mere human lover can. If a human being can eagerly long for his beloved so much, think of the depth of longing that God must have for those God loves.

In God's eyes, in the eyes of love, we are each and every one of us perfect. We are not perfect through our own merit, anymore than the bride was perfect through her own doing. We are not perfect by what we do or do not do, as the bride did not "do" anything to call forth the groom's acclamation of her perfection. She is perfect because in the love of the groom, she has been made perfect. Likewise we, as imperfect as we may be, are perfect in the love of God. Having made us perfect by love, God is anxious to join with us so that we may be made one with God.

Come with Me

Come with me from Lebanon, my bride;
    come with me from Lebanon.
Depart from the peak of Amana,

> from the peak of Senir and Hermon,
> from the dens of lions,
> from the mountains of leopards.
> *(4:8)*

Once again the groom calls the bride to come away with him. He calls her to come away from Lebanon, a place known for its finery. He calls her to leave the mountaintops. He calls her away from the places of danger, where lions and leopards dwell. She will have no need of the cedars of Lebanon when she is with him. She will have no need to climb mountains to find him. She will be saved from all danger in his presence.

God also continues to call us to come away. God calls us away from the distractions of Lebanon. We need not climb mountains to find God. We can leave all danger behind. God will provide all that we need. God will protect us. In God's presence, all else is extraneous.

God is calling us, "Come away."

Journal Questions

1. God finds beauty in each one of us. In your journal, list some of the ways in which you are beautiful. Allow yourself to look at yourself as God does, with eyes of love. What images might God use to describe your beauty?

2. What flaws do you see in yourself that make it difficult to believe that God wants to be united with you? What gets in the way of believing that God might see you as flawless?

3. Often we find places to hide from God. Sometimes they are physical places, but often they are other distractions. Keeping ourselves busy is a wonderful way to avoid intimacy with God. What mountains do you need to leave in order to spend time with God? What are the lions' dens that you need to depart?

Suggestions for Prayer

1. Read chapter 4, verses 1–5 slowly to yourself. If a word or phrase strikes you, stop and spend some time in silence listening. Allow God to tell you, through the passage, how beautiful you are.

2. If you have some flaw or sin that is troubling you and making it difficult for you to believe that God loves you, arrange a time for confession, either formally with a priest or minister or informally with a friend.

3. If you are using silence in your prayer, try to lengthen the time that you spend with your Lover. Either increase your time per encounter, or find additional times when you can heed the Groom's call to come away.

10

You Have Ravished My Heart

Song of Songs 4:9–5:1

How Sweet Is Your Love

You have ravished my heart, my sister, my bride,
>> you have ravished my heart with a glance of your eyes,
>> with one jewel of your necklace.
How sweet is your love, my sister, my bride!
>> how much better is your love than wine,
>> and the fragrance of your oils than any spice!
Your lips distill nectar, my bride;
>> honey and milk are under your tongue;
>> the scent of your garments is like the scent of Lebanon.
>>> *(4:9–11)*

Not only is the bride pining for the groom, but the groom is lovesick as well. Love is mutual, and the power of love is felt by both partners.

According to the groom, the bride has ravished his heart. He no longer controls it, for he has been overcome by the bride. "The lover's heart has been jolted, pushed around, and even taken without his consent."[46] A glance of her eyes is enough to command its surrender. Even one jewel of her necklace has an effect. He is wholly smitten. Her conquest is complete.

It is not simply a conquest, however, that the bride has won. It is not simply that the bride now has power over the groom. In other passages she makes it clear that she is equally smitten. She is in his power, as he is in hers—for when we give our hearts in love, they are no longer ours. Instead we joyfully hand them over to our beloved, knowing that we will never be satisfied until they rest in the beloved's presence always. Neither the bride nor the groom owns their own hearts. Their hearts are wholly owned by their lovers.

For the groom, the fruits of this surrender are clear. Her

love, the love that they share, is far better than the best wine. As he remembers their love, he remembers that which is most delectable about her. He remembers the way she smells; the perfumes she uses excite his imagination.

Her kisses are as sweet and pleasing as nectar. Her tongue tastes like milk and honey, the legendary fruits of the Promised Land—for in her arms he has indeed found his promised land. As she wraps her arms around him, he is enfolded in the scent of her garments. They remind him of the forests of Lebanon.

It is hard to imagine that God is smitten by us, hard to imagine God proclaiming that we have ravished God's heart. Yet how can we proclaim that God truly loves us unless we also acknowledge that we have the power to touch God? How can we proclaim that we are God's beloved if God is untouched by us? How can we truly enter into a love affair with one who does not passionately love us in return? Unrequited love turns bitter in the end. Only if the love is shared and fulfilled will it flower and blossom.

As hard as it may be to believe, God's heart is open to us, and we can ravish it. God's heart has been given to us so that we might in turn give our hearts fully to God. Our love, like the love of the bride for the groom, is better than wine and far sweeter than nectar, and God longs for the consummation of our love far more deeply and passionately than we can ever imagine.

A Garden Locked

A garden locked is my sister, my bride,
    a garden locked, a fountain sealed.
Your channel is an orchard of pomegranates
    with all choicest fruits,
    henna with nard,
nard and saffron, calamus and cinnamon,
    with all trees of frankincense,
myrrh and aloes,

with all chief spices—
a garden fountain, a well of living water,
and flowing streams from Lebanon.
   (4:12–15)

The picture the groom paints of the bride is a lovely one, but her delights are locked away, protected from any who might wish to enter. The bride is a garden full of delicious fruit, rich spices, and abundant water, but it is also a locked garden. She is like a fountain, but it is a sealed fountain. She is well protected from any who might want to gain unauthorized access to her delights.

The groom, however, knows what delights lie hidden behind the walls. Her garden has a whole orchard of pomegranates, a sign of fertility and life. She is bursting with fruit, fruit that he is longing to taste.

She is also blessed with an extravagant assortment of exotic spices, whose fragrance must have been overpowering when combined.[47] All the good things the groom can imagine are found in her garden. In that garden and that garden alone, he will find all that his heart can desire.

In the center of the garden is a fountain whose water cascades in a never-ending stream. In the garden is living water, the source of life and happiness for him. If only he could taste its fruit and drink of its water, he would finally be satisfied!

We also are precious gardens, filled with all manner of wonderful and costly things. In us is much to delight our Lover. God wishes to eat and drink deeply of the fruits of our garden.

Far too often, however, we lock the gates against God. We do not open up our hearts and our lives to our Lover. Far too often we keep God from entering the innermost parts of our garden, where God might enjoy the best that we have to offer.

God, however, knows what is in there. Our Lover is anxiously waiting for the gates to be opened and to be invited in. God could storm the gates, but that is not the way of love. Our Beloved will wait as long as necessary for us to open the gates, at least a crack—for a crack is all that God needs.

Blow Upon My Garden

Awake, O north wind,
  and come, O south wind!
Blow upon my garden
  that its fragrance may be wafted abroad.
Let my beloved come to his garden,
  and eat its choicest fruits.
I come to my garden, my sister, my bride;
  I gather my myrrh with my spice,
  I eat my honeycomb with my honey,
  I drink my wine with my milk.
Eat, friends, drink,
  and be drunk with love.
    (4:16—5:1)

The bride in her love, however, is not content with simply cracking open the gate slightly. She throws wide the gates, inviting in her lover. She even entreats the wind to help her bring the groom to where she wishes him to be. She calls on the north wind and the south wind to blow the fragrance of her garden to the beloved, that he might find his way to the garden and to her open gate.

She is waiting at the gate for his coming, and when he comes, she offers him the choicest fruits of the garden. All that she has, all that she is, she offers to him. Her only desire is that he enjoy all that she has prepared for him.

The groom, enticed by the wonderful smell, makes his way to the garden gate that the bride has flung wide for him. As he enters, the bride welcomes him, and he begins to enjoy all the garden's fruits. He gathers the rare spices and fills himself with the sweet smell of the garden. Eating the honey she provides, he delights in the sweetness of the garden. His thirst is quenched as he drinks deeply of the milk and the water.

Together he and the bride eat and drink until they are drunk on love, until they are filled to overflowing with their love for each other. Drunk with its sweetness, their love is consummated at last.

What will we do with our gardens? Will we keep them closed—safe and protected from all who might wish to enter? Will we keep them secret, allowing no one save ourselves to enter? Will we keep all their fruit for ourselves, or will we share them with our Beloved?

Like the bride, we are called to open wide our gates to let the Groom enter. We are called to let the sweet perfume of our garden entice God in. We are called to greet God, as our Beloved comes to the garden that we have specially prepared. We are to offer the fruits of the garden, that God might enjoy them.

It is no small thing to open wide our gates for God. When we do, we are vulnerable, unprotected. It requires a great deal of trust that the One who comes is the One who loves us and cares for us. It requires faith that we do not need to protect ourselves from our Lover any longer.

We may not be able to be quite as open, quite as blatant, or quite as welcoming as the bride in the Song of Songs. Over time we have learned to be cautious and protective of all that is really important to us, and nothing is more important to us than our inner gardens. We may be afraid that God will take over completely and we will be lost.

But the groom has no desire to enjoy the garden by himself. The lover is satisfied with the fruits of the garden only when his beloved is there with him. It is her presence that gives the garden all its special radiance. It is not the possession of the garden that is important to the groom, but the fulfilling of their love by sharing the garden with the bride.

We may not be able to open the gates of our gardens wide

right now. We may not even be aware of how tightly our gates are closed, thinking that the gates are already open when in truth they are still locked tight. We may need to rely on the winds to blow the sweet fragrance of the garden over our walls to our Beloved. We may have to listen for the knock at the gate. Our Lover, however, is waiting for us to dare to unlock the padlocks of our hearts.

When we do open the gates and invite God to join us, we will find a bliss that cannot be described. It is not only God who gets drunk on the fruits of the garden; we likewise will be drunk, drunk on the strong wine of our love of God.

Journal Questions

1. God is smitten with you. God is passionately in love with you. How does it make you feel to hear that? Can you believe that you have ravished God's heart? Why do you think such notions do or do not come easily to you?

2. Using art supplies, draw or make some representation of your garden. What would be in it and why? What fruit do you have to offer? What scents are the winds blowing to God— the delicate sweetness of flowers, the powerful scent of spices, or something else?

3. What makes it difficult for you to unlock the gates of your garden to God? What fears or worries keep you from throwing wide the gates of the garden and fully welcoming God into your garden?

Suggestions for Prayer

1. Use a term of endearment to center your prayer. Repeat it slowly over and over until you can rest in the silence, in God's presence. Allow God to communicate to you how passionately you are loved.

2. In your imagination, picture your garden. Make it as real as you can. Note what you see, what you hear, what you smell, what you can taste, and what you can touch. Fully immerse yourself in the image. Picture the gate standing wide open, and wait, ready to welcome God. Allow God to direct what will happen next, staying as open as possible to whatever God wishes to say to you.

3. Ask God to help you open your gates wider. Wait in silence for God to answer your prayer.

Chapter

11

I Sought Him, But Did Not Find Him

Song of Songs 5:2–7

Open to Me

I slept, but my heart was awake.
Listen! my beloved is knocking.
"Open to me, my sister, my love,
    my dove, my perfect one;
for my head is wet with dew,
    my locks with the drops of the night."
I had put off my garment;
    how could I put it on again?
I had bathed my feet;
    how could I soil them?

    (5:2–3)

Even in sleep the bride's ear was tuned to listen for her beloved. Though her mind slept, her heart was awake. In a dream he came to her.

The bride heard him knocking on the door. He was calling out to her, requesting permission to come in, for he was wet with the night's dew. He wanted shelter, shelter from the night, shelter in her arms. It was not that she was unmoved by his entreaties, for her heart leapt at the sound of his voice. Yet she did not immediately rise to let him in.

Instead she started debating about what she should do. She let her concerns and worries dull her response. It was not seemly for her to let him in, for she had already retired for the night. She was not dressed, and she could not answer his summons clothed only in her nightdress.

She had washed her feet, dirty from the day's traffic. To rise to meet he who stood at the door would dirty them again, and she did not wish to do that. She was clean and warm and comfortable, and as much as she loved him, her inertia won. She listened to his call, but she remained reclining on the couch, content with knowing that he desired her.

How often we make excuses to avoid spending time with God! As with the bride, God's calls to us may seem unreasonable at the time. God often appears at inconvenient times, upsetting the plans we have made. Like an importunate lover, God wishes to see us whenever God desires. God rarely makes appointments in advance!

We, like the bride, may have a whole set of reasons why we cannot attend to God at that moment when we feel God tugging at our hearts. We may think that we have all the time in the world. We may not want to be bothered. We may have more important business to conduct.

Yet if we claim that God is the most important thing in the world to us, surely our Beloved is worth the inconvenience. Surely, for God's sake, we can put aside our cares and concerns. Surely, for God's sake and the sake of the love that we share, we can rise at the sound of our Lover's voice and let God in.

I Called Him, But He Gave No Answer

> My beloved thrust his hand into the opening,
>   and my inmost being yearned for him.
> I arose to open to my beloved,
>   and my hands dripped with myrrh,
> my fingers with liquid myrrh,
>   upon the handles of the bolt.
> I opened to my beloved,
>   but my beloved had turned and was gone.
> My soul failed me when he spoke.
> I sought him, but did not find him;
>   I called him, but he gave no answer.
>   (5:4–6)

The groom does not give up easily. Knowing that the one he loves is inside, the groom tries his best to open the door of the place. He slides his hand into the opening by the door, hoping to be able to reach the latch that holds it firm, but he is unsuccessful. The door remains locked to him.

Listening to the efforts of the groom, the bride is finally moved to act. She feels a deep yearning, a longing for the one she loves. No longer do the excuses she has used seem adequate. Nothing is important now but that she go to the one who moves her heart by his presence.

She rises, still dressed for bed, still anointed from her bath, and moves swiftly to the door. The oil on her hands makes it difficult to draw the bolt. They slip, and she feels her longing grow ever deeper. At last the bolt gives way. At last she is able to throw open the door. At last she can welcome her lover.

She peers out in the darkness, but he is not there. Having tried all that he knew to open the door, he has finally given up. He has left, and she is alone in the night.

The desire and longing that had risen in response to his entreaties are painful reminders of what she has lost by her delays. She calls out to him. Maybe he is still within range of the sound of her voice. Though she cries repeatedly with all her heart and all her voice, there is no answer. She goes to the edge of the courtyard and cries even more, but still there is no answer. He is gone, and she is alone.

As the groom comes to the bride, so God comes to us. God calls out to us, asking to be let in. Our Lover tries to unlatch the doors of our heart. Like the groom, however, God will not batter down the doors. God will not force an entry. God needs to be invited in.

If we delay, we may find that when we are ready to greet our Lover, God is nowhere to be found. We may find that when we at last open the door, we will see no signs of the one for whom our hearts yearn. When we cry out to God, we may not hear an answer.

Having assumed that we had all the time in the world, we

may be appalled at the consequences of our inaction. Like the bride, we may become frantic. God is not at our beck and call. Having refused God's entreaties, it is now up to us to look for God.

They Wounded Me

Making their rounds in the city
   the sentinels found me;
they beat me, they wounded me,
   they took away my mantle,
   those sentinels of the walls.
     (5:7)

Throwing a mantle over her nightclothes, the bride rushes into the city, looking for her lover, but she has no idea where he has gone. Hoping for a glimpse of her lover, she hurries to the corner and peers around. There is no one in sight. She runs from place to place, frantically searching. All she knows is that the one who is everything to her has disappeared. She is close to despair, and her only hope is to find him, to redeem her refusal to open to him when he first called.

Running through the streets, crying out to him, she encounters the sentinels of the city. Dressed only in her mantle thrown over her nightclothes, they take her for a prostitute. No proper woman would be out alone at that time of night. They would all be in bed. No proper woman would ever be out dressed as she is dressed. The only ones who would dress that way would be women offering their bodies for sale. Such women have no protection.

She is not a prostitute, but they are right in thinking that she is not a proper woman. She has thrown away all sense of propriety in her search for the one she loves. Nothing matters anymore but the search for the beloved. She cares little what others say or think. She probably is unaware of her state of dress. She has no fears for her safety; her only fear is that she will never find him. She is completely vulnerable.

Being vulnerable, she has no defenses against the watchmen. They strip her mantle from about her, leaving her exposed in her nightclothes. They beat her and abuse her, and she has no protection against their violence. She is at their mercy.

Like the bride, when we feel that we have lost God, we may frantically look in hopes of finding our Lover. It is in times like those that we may try thing after thing, technique after technique, church after church in hopes that our Lover will be there.

Desperate for any glimpse of the Beloved, we may be lured into situations that are dangerous. The frantic searching can leave us open to being stripped and beaten and abused. We may allow others to abuse us, hoping that they can show us the way. It may be hard to know which way to go to find our Lover.

Our longing, our desire for God can indeed make us vulnerable, leaving us defenseless. It can leave us barely clothed in the chilly night of our fears and uncertainties. The search for God can be long, difficult, and painful. All that, however, will be of no consequence if we can at last find our Beloved.

Journal Questions

1. Like the bride, we are not always receptive to the entreaties of God to open our hearts. What excuses do you use to keep the door firmly latched against God?

2. When have you felt yourself deeply yearning for God? How did you respond to that longing?

3. Have there been times in your life when you called out to God and heard no answer? What did you do?

4. What places have you looked for God? Were any of them places of danger for you?

5. Searching for God can be a risky and dangerous business. Not all those we meet on our way will aid us in our search.

Think of the people you know. Who do you think might serve as a guide or companion in your search? Whom should you avoid?

6. In the midst of dark times, what keeps you from despair? If you are in the middle of a dark time, how can you gain access to those strengths and resources for your search?

Suggestions for Prayer

1. As you go through your day, be aware of signs that God may be calling you to open the doors of your heart. When you catch a glimpse or hear a whisper, stop and be attentive to what is going on. You may be surprised at what you hear.

2. Think of ways or places in which you have encountered God in the past. Return and spend some time in those ways or places listening for the voice of the Beloved.

3. In your prayer time, ask God to help you unlatch the doors of your heart so that you can respond to the Lover's voice whenever it may come.

4. If you are currently in a time of darkness and have no sense of God's presence, pray that God may guide your feet in your search and protect you as you wander the dark city streets.

Chapter

12

If You Find My Beloved

Song of Songs 5:8–16

I Am Faint with Love

I adjure you, O daughters of Jerusalem,
    if you find my beloved,
tell him this:
    I am faint with love.
What is your beloved more than another beloved,
    O fairest among women?
What is your beloved more than another beloved?
    that you thus adjure us?

    (5:8–9)

Before, when the bride had addressed the daughters of Jerusalem
in this way, it was to warn them. Repeatedly throughout the
Song, she warns them of the power and danger of love. She cau-
tions them not to stir things up until the right time. This time
something different happens.

She would now have a perfect excuse to warn them about the
dangers of love, the dangers of allowing yourself to be consumed
by passion. She is living proof of its dangers. Wandering the city
streets, desperate to find her lover, she had risked much for the
sake of her love, and her risk was not without consequences.
She encountered the night watchmen, and they beat and abused
her. Hurting and sore and discouraged, this would be a logical
place for her to insert another warning to the daughters of
Jerusalem. See what happened to me; make sure it doesn't happen to you. Wait for the right time and right place. Contain your
passion, or it will get you into trouble.

But educating the daughters of Jerusalem is not at the fore-
front of her mind. She is not interested in serving as an object
lesson. Despite all that has happened to her, she is still entirely
focused on finding her lover.

What is different this time is that she has lost the hope that she can do it on her own. She will need help, for she is at the end of her resources. Faint with love and the desperation of the search, she needs others to help her find him again. She, who once was the teacher of the daughters of Jerusalem, now turns to them for help. She will take help wherever she can find it. Maybe they can at least get a message to her beloved.

The women, however, are not initially sympathetic. Maybe they think she has made a fool of herself over this man. They call her fairest among women. Maybe they think she can do better than this man who keeps disappearing. Why should they help her find her beloved, since he has been trouble all along? There are plenty of other men in the world.

So the women challenge the bride. They challenge her to prove that he is worth it. They challenge her to show that he is superior to other men. They challenge her to prove that he is all that she says he is. Only when the bride proves that he is worth the effort will they join her in her efforts to find him.

Like the bride, battered and bruised in our attempts to find God, we may feel close to giving up. We also may feel that we are faint and in need of sustenance before we can continue on.

Like the bride, we may hope to find others who will support us in our search, or who may even search on our behalf. We may wish for someone who will bring God to us so that we no longer have to search the dark and dangerous streets. We may hope for others who can pass on our messages and speak on our behalf. Not all those we ask, however, will support our quest. Many will challenge it. Most will think we are wasting our time. Some will suggest other values and other pleasures that can be had far more easily. Many may suggest that we can find that for which we are searching in something or someone other than God.

It is a temptation to listen to those voices. When we are discouraged and faint, we may more easily be tempted to give up the search. We may be more willing to substitute someone or something else for God. The question often arises in such a time, "Is all this worth it?" We may believe so, but in difficult times, our faith can be shaken. When everyone else is questioning our love, it is difficult to remain focused on the Beloved and our search.

My Beloved Is All Radiant

My beloved is all radiant and ruddy,
    distinguished among ten thousand.
His head is the finest gold;
    his locks are wavy,
      black as a raven.
His eyes are like doves
    beside springs of water,
bathed in milk,
    fitly set.
His cheeks are like beds of spices,
    yielding fragrance.
His lips are lilies,
    distilling liquid myrrh.
His arms are rounded gold,
    set with jewels.
His body is ivory work,
    encrusted with sapphires.
His legs are alabaster columns,
    set upon bases of gold.
His appearance is like Lebanon,
    choice as the cedars.
      (5:10–15)

Challenged to defend her choice of lover, the bride rouses from her fainthearted state to launch into a passionate song of praise. It may be that he is elusive. It may be that she does not know where to find him. All that may be true, but it is also true that he is a lover beyond all compare.

This is no phantom lover whose outlines are barely discernable. This is no lover glimpsed only from a distance. This is the one she knows intimately, and whose body she can call to mind and describe so evocatively.

He is radiant, giving off light to those around him. By that, if nothing else, he is to be distinguished from all the others to whom the daughters of Jerusalem might choose to compare him. There is none like him. Even if he were in the midst of a great crowd of other men, even if there were ten thousand men, he would be unique, distinguished from all others.

How else is he to be distinguished? The bride begins her litany at the top of his head and works her way down. She describes the geography of her lover that she knows so well. His head glows like the finest gold, and his wavy locks are black as a raven. His dark eyes are like doves, and the whites are as bright and pure as milk. His cheeks yield their own fragrance. His lips, beautiful as lilies (the sign of their love), release their own intoxicating scent. His body is like a work of art. Arms of gold and jewels, body of ivory and sapphire, legs of alabaster, feet of gold— all come together in a vision of perfection, as tall and straight as a cedar of Lebanon.

It seems that the mere memory of her lover is enough to restore the bride. Through memory she is once again in his presence. Through memory she is rescued from her fainthearted- ness. As the description goes on, you can almost hear her energy returning. She is ready once again to seek her lover, with or without the help of the daughters of Jerusalem!

Like the bride, we encounter times when it seems that we cannot go on. There are times when we no longer seem to have the energy to continue our search, to continue our struggle, and there are times when we wait passively for something to happen to us.

It is in those times that the memories of our experiences of God become vitally important. They can restore and re-energize us. Like the bride, remembering, really remembering those moments can be the gift we need to continue our search.

We may have one particular moment that stands out in our memory, some time when we were vividly aware of God's presence. Or we may have several smaller, quieter moments, but each of us has at some point been in the presence of God.

We may not have labeled those moments as being in God's presence at the time. Each of us, though, has those moments when we are transfixed by beauty or awed by some miracle or strangely warmed and comforted or inspired by grandeur. Whether we acknowledge it or not, in those moments we are being touched by God's Spirit, and those memories have the power to restore our souls.

This Is My Beloved

> His speech is most sweet,
>> and he is altogether desirable.
> This is my beloved and this is my friend,
>> O daughters of Jerusalem.
>> *(5:16)*

There is a reason for her willingness to endure danger, the bride triumphantly proclaims. There is a reason that she is unwilling to give up the search, no matter how long it takes. He is different and altogether desirable.

Summing up the qualities of her beloved, the bride remembers the sweetness of his speech. The sound of his voice has been enough to rouse her. It is surpassingly sweet in her ears.

Surely the daughters of Jerusalem can now see that he is not simply another man, with his own set of faults and flaws. Just as the groom has proclaimed her perfect, the bride now returns the compliment. As thrilling as each part of him is individually, the totality is more. He is altogether desirable.

Most important of all, he is hers. He is her friend and her

beloved. Even if he were not radiant, even if his form were not perfect, even if his voice were not sweet, he would still surpass all others, for she has claimed him.

No description that we can give of our Lover does God justice. We can describe certain aspects of God. We can recount what we have experienced. We can relate what others have passed on. Yet like the bride, at some point we will have to say that our description pales in comparison to our Beloved. It catches only the faintest glimpse of the glory of the One we love. Like the groom, God is altogether desirable. God is the source of all desire, and it is only God who can in the end satisfy our desires.

Like the bride, however, we are not meant to be passive in our relationship. We are meant to claim God as our own, even as we have been claimed by God. It sounds audacious to claim God as ours, and yet only when we do so can we really give our heart to God.

To claim a lover as our own is to deny the claims of any other lover. To claim a lover as our own is to set our heart firmly on one, and only one, beloved. To claim our lover as our own is to commit ourselves fully.

It is not easy to do that. It is scary to fall in love. It means that we leave all other sources of security. Are we really willing to claim God as our Beloved and our Friend, all that we need? Only the power of love and the desirability of the Beloved can give us the courage we need.

Journal Questions

1. What are the voices that challenge you to give up your search for God and settle for another lover? Have they ever convinced you to abandon your search?

2. Think of a time when you have felt God's presence. Describe

it in as much detail as you can. Record what you saw, felt, and heard. What does this memory tell you about God? How would you describe to others the God portrayed in that memory?

3. What fears do you have about claiming God as your Beloved, your Friend? What parts of your life would you be reluctant to commit fully to God?

Suggestions for Prayer

1. Spend some time thinking about the ways in which you have been hurt in your search for God. What bruises, sprains, wounds, or broken bones remain? After you have uncovered them, ask God to begin healing them. Spend some time in silence, being open to God's healing Spirit.

2. God is present with us all the time, but often we are so distracted that we do not see the signs. Becoming aware of God in all of our life is known as practicing the presence of God. Although we will never be aware of God at every moment, we can become more aware of God. One exercise that helps is to pick an object or a place that you will see every day (preferably multiple times a day). Whenever you see it, remind yourself to call God to mind. You do not need to spend a long time in these remembrances. Even a short period of silence can enhance the sense of God's presence in your life. The more you practice it, the more you will be open to recognizing God's hand at work in your life.

3. In your centering prayer time, use the words "My Beloved" or "My Friend" to focus your prayer. Allow yourself to begin to claim that exclusive relationship with God.

Chapter

13

I Am My Beloved's and My Beloved Is Mine

Song of Songs 6:1–3

That We May Seek Him with You

Where has your beloved gone,
  O fairest among women?
Which way has your beloved turned,
  that we may seek him with you?

  (6:1)

There is a change in the daughters of Jerusalem. Originally when the bride asked for their help to find her lover, they were uninterested, even scornful. They did not see why she should bother with him. They believed there was nothing special about this man. They challenged her to explain to them why they should care.

In an outburst of praise and adoration, the bride did just that. She filled their ears with the sound of her love, vividly picturing his glory for all to see. She was carried off by the sheer remembrance of him, and in her rapture, the daughters of Jerusalem have also been moved.

No longer do the women wish to sit idly while she searches. They, too, now desire to see the beloved. They want to find the one about whom they have heard so much. They are eager to join her in her search.

"Where should we start looking?" they ask. "Where did you last see him?" "Which direction was he heading?" "Give us some guidance, so that we may also look." The groom has begun to attract others besides the bride.

When we are in love with God, our enthusiasm will affect those around us. Who does not wish the kind of joy that comes with being in love? Who does not wish to find the One who will make our heart sing the way the groom made the bride's heart sing?

In the end we may not get help from others in finding God, but if we are open and honest about what we have found, others may begin to follow us as we search. Others may join us, not as a favor or a help to us, but because they are looking for that which we have already found. Love and joy are contagious and very alluring.

Gone Down to His Garden

My beloved has gone down to his garden,
>   to the beds of spices,
to pasture his flock in the gardens,
>   and to gather lilies.
>>   *(6:2)*

After all her searching, after all her adventures, after all her pleas for help from others, the beloved is finally found. In the end it is not the bride's efforts that yield results. She did not find him. In the end it would be the beloved who would find her.

She tells the daughters of Jerusalem that he has gone down into his garden, but it is not some literal garden. At the beginning of chapter 5, the groom described his bride as a garden. Just before that the bride also described herself as a garden. She asked the wind to entice him into her garden. Suddenly he is there. The groom has found the garden that she has so lovingly prepared for him. They are finally together, and she no longer needs the help of the daughters of Jerusalem.

Her garden was earlier described as a veritable cornucopia of spices. Henna, nard, saffron, calamus, cinnamon, frankincense, myrrh, aloes—all these are found in the garden prepared and waiting for him. He is there among the beds of spices. In coming to the garden, he is surrounded, perhaps overwhelmed, by the intoxicating smell of their love.

The bride is not coyly refusing to let others know of his presence, but is indeed trumpeting his return, using the earlier images of their love. All that she had wished to happen is now happening. He has taken up residence in the garden, pasturing his flock there. Most of all, he is gathering the lilies, a continuing symbol of their love.

We can and we need to search for God. Those in love are compelled to look high and low for the one they love. Nothing else seems to really matter when we are separated from the One we love.

Often, however, love seems to come to us, not as a result of our search or our efforts, but simply as a gift. It may appear long after we have given up all hope. It may appear in an unexpected place or a strange way.

Sometimes we find God where we expect, but often that is not the case. We can go to places where we have found God previously, without success. We can follow the paths that others have described, with disappointing results. We can even lapse into despair, having searched everywhere, for God can be elusive.

Sometimes it is only when we have given up hope of accomplishing it ourselves that God appears to us. Without warning we may be flooded with a sense of God's presence, and suddenly know that God has entered our garden. Those are God's gifts to us, times to be enjoyed, savored, and most of all, remembered. The love we share is real, but like any love, it is not predictable. It is all the more powerful because we experience both the rapture of presence and the pain of absence. The presence reminds us of why we pursue our lover, and the absence sharpens our desire. When God comes to you, gather lilies together and share the incredible sweetness of your love!

My Beloved Is Mine

I am my beloved's and my beloved is mine;
    he pastures his flock among the lilies.

    (6:3)

In the rapture of the beloved's presence, the bride realizes a new and compelling truth. It is something that has been a theme throughout the Song, but in that moment, it comes to the surface in a more compelling way. In the time they share in the garden, they are brought together in a new and more profound way. They are joined, and the bride can proclaim that theirs is a relationship that will supersede all others.

I am my beloved's, the bride says. No longer can she claim simply to be her own. There is one who has an even deeper claim on her. She has been claimed, completely, utterly. She belongs to another.

It is not simply, however, that the groom owns her. There is mutuality in this relationship. Even as she acknowledges his claim on her, she launches into her own claim on him. She may belong completely to the groom, but the reverse is also true. The beloved is hers. He has been claimed just as firmly, just as completely as she has been claimed.

It is this claiming of each other that allows their love to grow and flourish. It is this that marks the depth of their love. It is this that makes it possible for the beloved to pasture his flocks among the lilies of their love. Love requires such mutuality.

At some point in our relationship with God, we will also feel that we have truly been claimed. We will begin to realize that God has indeed claimed us for God's own. If we are not able to respond with like passion, such a love can seem confining, even threatening. We may wish for an escape, or at least a little more freedom. We do not like to acknowledge that we are owned by another.

If, however, we can get past our worries and fears and respond in love to that love, then we will be transformed. We will begin to experience that sense of claim or ownership as reciprocal. We will then be able to claim God as our own as well.

When we are able to participate fully in that exchange, our love will have a chance to grow and flourish in new and deeper ways. We will have a greater sense of God's presence with us. And we will know what it is like for God to pasture God's flock among the lilies of our love.

Journal Questions

1. Think of times when others have turned to you for help in their relationship with God. How have you helped lead them toward the Beloved? What in particular did you say or do that attracted others to the search for God?

2. Think of times when you have been surprised by a sense of awe, wonder, or God's presence. Are there any common factors in those times? Which ones were you prepared for, and which ones were pure gifts of grace?

3. Was there a time in your life when you felt that God had claimed you? What was your response? Can you now claim God as your own? Why or why not?

Suggestions for Prayer

1. Spend some time in silence, allowing the names of those around you to come to mind. Which of those people are currently seeking God? Ask God to help you find a way to share your journey with them.

2. Ask God to open your eyes to see God's presence in unexpected places. Look carefully for signs of God's presence in every place that you find yourself. Expect to find God wherever you go.

3. If you do not feel that God has claimed you, ask God to help you feel that now. Spend some time in silence, allowing God to respond to your request.

4. If you have a sense that God has claimed you, spend some time praying that you may be able to claim God as your own. Spend some time in centering prayer, using the phrase "You are mine."

5. If you are already comfortable claiming God as your own, pray that God may pasture God's flocks among your lilies. Spend time in silence, waiting for the coming of the Beloved.

14

My
Perfect
One

Song of Songs 6:4–12

For They Overwhelm Me

You are beautiful as Tirzah, my love,
    comely as Jerusalem,
    terrible as an army with banners.
Turn away your eyes from me,
    for they overwhelm me!
Your hair is like a flock of goats,
    moving down the slopes of Gilead.
Your teeth are like a flock of ewes,
    that have come up from the washing;
all of them bear twins,
    and not one among them is bereaved.
Your cheeks are like halves of a pomegranate
    behind your veil.

    (6:4–7)

Again the groom bursts into praise for the beauty of the bride. She is as beautiful as Tirzah, a renowned metropolis.[48] She is as comely as Jerusalem. There is, however, a dangerous side to her beauty, for it is also as terrible as an army with banners flying.

She incites in the groom that same fear a soldier feels when a large and well-equipped army begins to head his way. Banners blowing in the breeze, it announces itself from the distance. With no hope of retreat and little hope of prevailing, all the soldier can do is wait for the onslaught. It is a magnificent and yet terrible sight.

Likewise the groom has no hope of retreat. He is held fast in the bride's gaze. Her eyes hold him motionless, like a deer caught in the headlights of an oncoming car. He cannot tear himself away. He is wholly at her mercy.

His only hope is that she will indeed be merciful. His only hope is that she will release him from the hold that she has on him, for all his defenses have been overwhelmed. "Turn away your eyes," he pleads.

Although he asks to be released, I do not think that freedom would satisfy him for long. He is as hopelessly in love as the bride is. Although he may approach her with fear and trembling, to leave would be even worse.

He does not launch into further entreaties to be released, but instead repeats his praise of her beauty in the same images he has used before. They may not adequately express her loveliness, but love seeks expression in words, no matter how inadequate. Those words become their words, the words they share with each other. By repetition they become hallowed.

God yearns for us every bit as much and as passionately as the groom yearns for his beloved. God finds us as beautiful as the groom finds the beloved. Does God find us as terrible? Do we really hold such power over God?

God has given us tremendous power. God has entrusted us with all that is most precious. We have been given the creation to love and care for. We have been given the people around us: our families, friends, and communities. In the Christian tradition, God even entrusted God's Son to us. That is an enormous amount of power.

Why would God give all this to us, particularly when we have not always had a good track record? Why would God choose to allow us this power, when often we have not used our power wisely? It does not make sense.

It makes sense only if God loves us, really loves us, for allowing yourself to be vulnerable is a part of what it means to love. God had no need to love us. God was complete without our love, but in choosing to love, God became vulnerable. What we do, what we say, and the love we express—they all matter to God. God has allowed us to hold God captive in love. Such a love calls forth love in return. It demands a response. Are we willing to risk loving God as God loves us?

The Only One

There are sixty queens and eighty concubines,
> and maidens without number.
My dove, my perfect one, is the only one,
> the darling of her mother,
> flawless to her that bore her.
The maidens saw her and called her happy;
> the queens and concubines also, and they praised her.
"Who is this that looks forth like the dawn,
> fair as the moon, bright as the sun,
> terrible as an army with banners?"
> *(6:8–10)*

Even in the midst of a great multitude of women, the bride stands out. The groom compares the bride with the whole of the king's harem. In the harem are gathered the cream of the cream. There one would find the women of noble birth. There one would find the most beautiful women of the country. Even among this select group of beautiful and noble women, the bride is unique.

Every other woman has some sort of imperfection. Only the bride is completely without flaw. She is the perfect one, the only one. She is flawless.

Of course, one would expect a lover to say this. Lovers are notoriously blind to the flaws of the one they love. We could dismiss it as simply the hyperbole of love.

The groom, however, protests that it is not simply he who knows this to be true. Even the other women agree that the bride is unique. The maidens called her happy. The queens and the concubines also praised her. Even among their great beauty, she was something to behold.

When he looks at her, the groom is reminded of the bright

beauty of the dawn. She shines like the sun in brightness, and she is as beautiful as the moon.

He acknowledges that this beauty is not simply something to be enjoyed, but a powerful force with which he must reckon. Again he repeats that it is as terrible as an army with banners!

There is a glow in the faces of those who have found the love of God. It is like the glow of those who have just fallen in love. They are indeed beautiful. Even if their features were plain in the beginning, love transforms them into something special. Brides on their wedding day radiate such beauty.

So do the lovers of God. When they are loved and when they give themselves in love, they are indeed as fair as the moon. When they are loved and when they give themselves in love, they shine as brightly as the sun. Such a glow holds power and strength. Such people attract and hold us captive, as an army holds prisoners.

Before I Was Aware

I went down to the nut orchard,
  to look at the blossoms of the valley,
to see whether the vines had budded,
  whether the pomegranates were in bloom.
Before I was aware, my fancy set me
  in a chariot beside my prince.

Signs of the spring are all around her. Eager for the return of spring, she has gone in search of evidence to indicate that it has come at last. She has gone to the nut orchard, to look at the blossoms of the valley, to fill her eyes with the sight of their beauty and fill her nose with the sweetness of their scent.

She hoped that there would be other signs as well. Maybe the grapevines would have blossomed. Maybe the pomegranates were in bloom. Maybe she could rejoice in their new life, even as she rejoiced in the new life that she now shared with her beloved.

Spring and lovers are drawn to each other. After winter, when little grows and all seems quiet and dead, spring breaks through extravagantly. The sights and smells appear almost overnight, overwhelming all that is dead or dormant.

So it is also with love. The extravagance that is a part of spring is also a part of love. Love is not content to give only what is necessary, but it seeks to cover all with its blossoms. The joy and abundance of life reflected in lovers' eyes are aptly captured in the abundance of spring.

Enjoying the fruits of spring is no substitute in the bride's mind for the lover. It can, however, sustain her in her wait for his coming. She can enjoy the beauty of creation while musing on the even greater beauty of the one she loves.

The beauty of spring seems to work its magic. For a moment at least, she is distracted enough that she does not hear the approach of her lover. He comes upon her suddenly, and she is overwhelmed and captured. Intent on another task, she is suddenly brought into her lover's presence.

Our love for God may make us, like the bride, more attuned to the beauty of the world around us. The new life that such a love brings to us may make us more aware of the way in which new life is bubbling up all around us. Like the bride, we may go looking for such signs as a way of celebrating our new life in God, even as we await our Lover's visit.

In such moments we may lose ourselves in the beauty. In such a loss of our normal self-consciousness, we may be more open to the presence of God. Like the bride, we may suddenly be overwhelmed by God's presence and our hearts may be captured. For such beauty is one of God's great gifts to us, and our Lover's gifts often have the power to summon the Giver to our presence.

Journal Questions

1. Spend some time thinking about your life. What kinds of decisions are you called to make about how you live your life? Over what areas has God given you power? What does that tell you about God?

2. What areas of your life do you resist giving up to God? What would need to happen for you to be willing to be vulnerable in those areas?

3. Think of people in your life who you have felt radiated a sense of God's love. What was their effect on those around them?

4. Think of a time when you have unexpectedly felt you were in the presence of God. Was there something about that time that might have enabled you to be more open to God's Spirit?

Suggestions for Prayer

1. Spend some time in prayer, asking God to help you be vulnerable to your Lover, as God has been vulnerable to you.

2. Thank God for all those who have radiated God's love in your life. Pray that you may radiate God's love toward all whom you encounter.

3. Spend some time in an activity in which you can fully lose yourself. Such a loss of self can also be a form of prayer.

15

How Fair
and
Pleasant
You
Are

Song of Songs 6:13–7:9

Return, That We May Look Upon You

Return, return, O Shulammite!
Return, return, that we may look upon you.
Why should you look upon the Shulammite,
as upon a dance before two armies?

(6:13)

This is the only place in the Song of Songs that identifies the woman in any way. The term *Shulammite,* however, is mysterious, although there have been various suggestions about its origin. In any case, it is a term used not by the woman herself or even by the groom, but by those in attendance upon her and the groom. What terms they use for each other remain a secret.

The attendants cry out to see more of the woman. They want her to perform for them, to provide some entertainment. She, however, demurs. She is not a spectacle like that of two armies jousting with each other. She may be willing to dance, but she dances not for their amusement but as a gift to the one she loves.

People often want us to perform for them. They demand that we fulfill their expectations. They expect us to prove ourselves.

Like the bride, however, we can refuse to do it. We do not have to impress others. We do not have to prove ourselves, for if we are loved and valued, the opinions of others are of little importance. They can demand all they want, but we will save our best for our Lover!

A King Is Held Captive in the Tresses

How graceful are your feet in sandals,
O queenly maiden!

> Your rounded thighs are like jewels,
> the work of a master hand.
> Your navel is a rounded bowl
> that never lacks mixed wine.
> Your belly is a heap of wheat,
> encircled with lilies.
> Your two breasts are like two fawns,
> twins of a gazelle.
> Your neck is like an ivory tower.
> Your eyes are pools in Heshbon,
> by the gate of Bath-rabbim.
> Your nose is like a tower of Lebanon,
> overlooking Damascus.
> Your head crowns you like Carmel,
> and your flowing locks are like purple;
> a king is held captive in the tresses.
> (7:1–5)

The bride has no objection to dancing. Dancing for her is a joy when it is done for the one she loves. In that case it becomes not a way to prove herself but a gift that she gives to her lover. Knowing that her audience is the one who has already pledged his love, she can give herself to the dance unself-consciously.

It must have been a marvelous exhibition, for it sends the groom into another round of praise. He praises her for her grace in the dance. He is captivated by her movements, and her feet in her sandals are objects to be admired.

This is no ordinary dance, and it is well that the Shulammite refused to do it in front of the attendants. This is not a state dance but an intimate dance, suitable only for lovers. No longer hidden behind concealing clothes, the bride is fully revealed to the groom. This is a dance for him, and for him alone.

Beginning this time with the feet, the graceful feet that first attracted his attention, the groom feasts his eyes on his beloved and rejoices in the beauty that has been revealed to him. Her thighs are smooth and polished, as the costliest of gems are shaped by the hands of the craftsman to show forth their hidden beauty.

He continues upward, marveling at her beauty. Her navel is like a rounded bowl, full of the most delicious wine, wonderful to the taste. Her belly is a mound of gold, like that of wheat, surrounded by lilies, the symbol of their love. Her breasts are perfectly matched, as twin gazelle fawns.

Still continuing upward, he is entranced by her beauty. Her neck is long, white, and smooth, like a tower of ivory. Her eyes are dark and deep like the pools of water at Heshbon. Her nose is as straight and majestic as one of the towers of Lebanon. Crowning it all is her head, towering over all the way that Mount Carmel towers over the land. Her hair with its glinting highlights is a marvel to behold, capturing the lover in its locks. The gift of herself, fully given, is indeed powerfully attractive.

Like the bride, we are called to uncover ourselves in God's presence, to allow all that we have used to hide ourselves to drop away. Like the bride, we are called to come into God's presence hiding nothing from our Lover.

We may be frightened to do so, afraid of what God might think if we were that exposed. We may be ashamed and wish like Adam and Eve to hide our vulnerability. We may simply be shy in the presence of our Lover.

Like the bride, however, we are called to dance in the presence of God. We dance not for the sake of those who command us to dance. We dance for our Lover, as our gift to God. We uncover our true selves, not so that we can be ashamed or embarrassed, but so that God can delight in our beauty as well. We are beautiful in the eyes of God, for God sees us with the eyes of love. Love chooses to see not the flaws but the glory of the one who is loved. God loves us deeply and passionately. We have nothing to fear as we uncover ourselves for our Beloved, for God is prepared to be captivated by us.

I Will Climb the Palm Tree

How fair and pleasant you are,
　　O loved one, delectable maiden!
You are stately as a palm tree,
　　and your breasts are like its clusters.
I say I will climb the palm tree
　　and lay hold of its branches.
Oh, may your breasts be like clusters of the vine,
　　and the scent of your breath like apples,
and your kisses like the best wine
　　that goes down smoothly,
　　gliding over lips and teeth.
　　　　(7:6–9)

As beautiful as the bride is to look at, the beloved is not content with simply looking. He wants a deeper experience of his beloved.

The images used here are of smell and taste. Throughout the book those senses have been an important element in the growing love relationship. Spices and wine have had a special place. Now the groom is ready to taste the pleasures that the bride has promised him, for she is delectable!

He starts out with a description of her looks, a continuation of the previous verses. She is stately, stately as a palm tree. Her breasts are like the clusters of the fruit of the palm. The descriptions soon lead him to imagine how it is that he might come to possess his beloved in a more intimate way.

What is one to do with a tree whose fruit hangs temptingly out of reach? Why, climb it, of course! So it is that the groom changes from merely describing the physical aspect of the beloved to contemplating how his desire might be fulfilled.

The comparison of her breasts to the fruit of the palm leads to other comparisons. Maybe they are less like dates and more like grapes. Like grapes, they are juicy and sweet. Her breath is also sweet. It is like the scent of apples.

Speaking of her breath reminds him of the kisses of her mouth. He saves the fullest description for those kisses. They are wonderful beyond all imagining. They are not simply like wine, but like the best wine. They are smooth and sweet, gliding over teeth and lips. They are like wine that slides smoothly down your throat and sets you on fire as it descends. So the kisses of the bride affect the groom. Earlier on, it is the bride who seemed most consumed with passion. In this section it is clear that the groom is equally enthralled and entranced.

It is somehow easier to imagine God as passionless, beyond the passions that stir our souls, and yet we believe that we are made in the image and likeness of God. God has made us to be passionate creatures; could we dare to believe that in our passionate desires, we might be reflecting the very passion of God?

Can we dare to believe that God desires to enter into a more intimate relationship with us? Could it be that God is not content with simply observing us from afar but wishes to draw ever nearer? Can we imagine God wanting to enjoy what we have to offer?

It is a startling thought, particularly if we have been raised in a tradition that has emphasized the transcendence of God over God's immanence, God's distance as opposed to God's nearness. The biblical tradition speaks of both as necessary for understanding the reality of God. For at least a time, can we really imagine God desiring to be intimate with us?

Journal Questions

1. All of us have expectations placed on us by others. Spend some time listing those expectations. Which expectations lead you into paths of love? Which ones are harmful? What do you need to do to free yourself from the expectations of others that are not helpful?

2. Who do you feel the most need to impress? How would your life change if your energy was refocused on impressing God?

3. Often we have events in our past that make us ashamed. What things do you try to hide from others? from yourself? from God?

4. We each need to experience God as both immanent and transcendent. How do you experience God most vividly? Is God transcendent (majestic, powerful, distant) or immanent (close, comforting, present) in those experiences? Can you think of times when you have experienced the other side of God?

5. Imagine God enjoying you. What would God most enjoy about you?

Suggestions for Prayer

1. Use the list of expectations from journal question 1. Spend some time in silence praying about each one, asking God to help you discern which of those expectations you are being called to honor.

2. Find a place where you will not be observed or disturbed, and dance for God. Do not worry about what it looks like or if it is right. Simply move your body in a way that seems to express your love of God.

3. Slowly read chapter 7, verses 1–9, savoring each verse. Listen for God's desire for you in the verses. Spend some time in silence, allowing the words to continue to echo in your heart.

Chapter

16

There I Will Give You My Love

Song of Songs 7:10–8:4

The Mandrakes Give Forth Fragrance

I am my beloved's,
    and his desire is for me.
Come, my beloved,
    let us go forth into the fields,
    and lodge in the villages;
let us go out early to the vineyards,
    and see whether the vines have budded,
whether the grape blossoms have opened
    and the pomegranates are in bloom.
There I will give you my love.
The mandrakes give forth fragrance,
    and over our doors are all choice fruits,
new as well as old,
    which I have laid up for you, O my beloved.
    (7:10–13)

The bride and the groom are well matched, passion for passion. Throughout the book we have seen their level of desire rise. First to be affected was the bride, but in the last chapter, the groom also showed that he was able to match her passion. When both reach such heights, the only possible outcome seems to be fulfillment, the consummation of their love.

So it is that the bride pictures the place and the way in which the two lovers will at last share the passion that is burning so deeply within them. The fulfillment of their deepest desires seems to be close at hand.

As the natural world has been so much a part of their courtship and their love, she imagines giving him her love outside. Only the beauty of nature can properly complement the beauty of their love, and what place is more fitting than the vineyard? Throughout this book their love has been compared to the finest wine. In the midst of the grape blossoms, they will fulfill their love.

There are, however, other plants that play a part in her imagined union. The pomegranate also figures in this scene. Earlier in the book, the groom compares the red curve of her cheek to the fruit of the pomegranate. In this piece the bride is looking for the bloom of the pomegranate plant, that first step in the plant's ability to put on fruit.

The pomegranate fruit, full of small seeds, has often been used as a sign of fertility. The union of bride and groom leads to their fertility, as the blossoms of the pomegranate plant leads to its fertility. The fertility image is enhanced by the allusion to the mandrake. The mandrake plant was used as both an aphrodisiac and an enhancer of fertility.[49]

The joining together of the bride and groom, then, is not simply for their pleasure and their joy, although it is clear from all that has occurred in this book that it will indeed be a pleasure and a joy. The joining together of the bride and groom is meant to be fruitful as well. As the pomegranate is bursting with the seeds of new life, so the union of the two lovers will result in new life.

In that union, all that the bride has to offer will be united with her lover. All that she has stored up will be sampled, tasted, and ultimately transformed. Nothing will be held back, no reserves, for everything she desired will be hers in that moment.

Our ever-deepening relationship with God brings us great pleasure and great joy. That is one of the gifts God gives us, to lure us ever deeper in love. The end result, however, is not simply to bring us joy. Our relationship with God is meant to be fruitful. It is meant to overflow the bounds of the individual relationship with God and to touch and transform those who come into contact with the lovers.

That is, in the end, how we tell whether the relationship we are pursuing is really with God. We can tell by the effects it has on those around us. We can tell by the way in which it affects our behavior. We can tell by the fruit it bears. Union with God produces much beautiful fruit.

If we wish to unite with God, we will need to make an offering of all that we have and all that we are. That is the soil we offer for the planting of God's word. In that fertile ground, God's love can grow and flourish, and such growth blesses all who draw near.

No One Would Despise Me

O that you were like a brother to me,
    who nursed at my mother's breast!
If I met you outside, I would kiss you,
    and no one would despise me.
I would lead you and bring you
    into the house of my mother,
      and into the chamber of the one who bore me.
I would give you spiced wine to drink,
    the juice of my pomegranates.
    (8:1–2)

Love has difficulty observing proprieties. It resists being contained. It yearns to overflow all boundaries. The bride yearns to be able to express publicly all that she is feeling.

The bride knows that what she wants is scandalous and that others will condemn her for any public display of her love. She knows that what she wants is not proper, but oh, how she longs for their love to be out in the open. Oh, how she longs to be able to greet her lover without restraint. How she longs to be free to declare her love in the streets.

The only man on whom the bride could publicly bestow such affection would be a brother. She could kiss her brother in the streets, and no one would chastise her. She would not need to restrain her natural impulses. The bride wishes that she could share that intimacy with her beloved, and even the deeper intimacy that is shared between twins. Twins have a bond fostered while nursing side-by-side that cannot be broken, and that bond, unlike the bond of romantic love, is acceptable even on the city streets.

She could lead her brother back to their house, and no one would object. They could spend time alone together, and no one would find anything to comment on. She could serve him, and all would praise her for being a loving and dutiful sister. If only she could do the same with her beloved!

Our pursuit of God can also seem scandalous to others. To approach God with a dutiful love is still acceptable. It is all right to go to church, as long as we do not get carried away. Proprieties must be observed there at all costs.

Passion, on the other hand, is often suspect. Throughout the centuries religious establishments have recognized that direct and passionate union with God is not something easily controlled. At times, in ecstasy, people have wandered off into strange and unhelpful ideas about God and themselves. Some have given themselves airs. Others have declared themselves to be God. Passion does not always lead to appropriate outcomes.

So it is that passion is circumscribed in most cultures, including that of the Church. Proprieties are enforced, often rigidly. Dutiful love is often preached and taught more than passionate love. Things done out of duty are praised, but those done out of passion are usually questioned.

In the midst of such demands, it is sometimes easier to hide, to pretend that our love is of some other kind. We may pretend that we are motivated by duty, when we are on fire with passion. We may pretend that our Lover is really our brother, in order that we may be allowed to be alone with God. The bride knows how much easier it is to escape the eyes of the censors if we at least pretend to abide by the rules.

Do Not Stir Up or Awaken Love

O that his left hand were under my head,
   and that his right hand embraced me!
I adjure you, O daughters of Jerusalem,
   do not stir up or awaken love
   until it is ready!
   (8:3–4)

In the end, however, the fiction of "brotherly" love will not prove satisfactory to the bride. She wants more, so much more than is allowed even with a sibling or a twin. Only the intimacies of lovers will do!

It is her repeated refrain. She wants to be held close. She wants the embrace of her lover. It is her fervent wish in chapter 2, and it is repeated again here. Again she is filled with that longing for the bliss she can only know in her lover's arms. She could, in that embrace, find all that she so passionately desires.

It is no nice, sweet longing that she experiences, but a raging passion. Again she warns the women of Jerusalem to be careful. Passion, such as she has for the groom, is not something to be trifled with, for it has the power to completely consume. If they stir it up, they will not be able to control it any better than she can. Such passion is overwhelming.

Pursuing such a love is indeed a risky business. It is not for the fainthearted. Many a book has been written about the power of passion in human relationships and the way in which we can be overpowered by our passion.

If such is true in human relationships, what about our relationship with God? Is it really safe? The answer from lovers of God throughout human history is no. It is not safe. God has often been pictured as a raging fire, a violent thunderstorm, and an earthquake. All those images have within them an acknowledgment of the wildness and unpredictability of God. All of them remind us that God cannot be controlled.

Do we dare enter into the whirlwind with Jonah? Do we dare jump into the raging sea with Peter? Do we dare, like Abraham, to venture into unknown territory to follow God?

If we have been pulled into a passionate relationship with God, then the answer must indeed be yes. Any other answer would be incomprehensible to the bride, who longs only to feel the arms of her lover encircling her. We have no promise of safety, but we do have the promise that in our Lover's arms, we will find all that our hearts desire. Are we ready to awaken our love?

Journal Questions

1. In what ways has your deepening relationship with God borne fruit? What effect has your life with God had on your relationships with those around you? Has your love for God overflowed onto others?

2. If you had to describe the soil in which God's word has been planted in you, what would you say? In what ways could your soil be enriched so that it bears more fruit?

3. What support do you have from your church, your family, and your friends for deepening your relationship with God? Do you feel a need to hide the depth of your feelings for God from those around you?

4. When you think of God's power, what images come to mind? Draw or sculpt your image of God. Spend time considering what it means to fall in love with a Lover of such great power.

Suggestions for Prayer

1. Allow yourself to imagine a place where you could give your love to God. Fill it with objects that symbolize what is best

about your relationship. Once you have furnished it, invite God to join you there. Spend time in silence awaiting your Lover.

2. In your quiet time, bring forward names of people you know who are in need of God's love and concern. Allow their names to rest in the love you share with God. Ask God to help you share God's love with them.

3. Ask God to help you to find other ways of relating to God that pass by the censors in your life, whether they are family, members of your faith community, friends, or even your internal censor. Spend some time alone with God, where you do not have to worry about the reactions of others.

4. Job encounters God in a whirlwind. Imagine God present to you in a whirlwind or another natural phenomenon of great power. Notice your reaction to imagining God in this way. What feelings does it generate? Ask God to help you enter the whirlwind (or other phenomenon) so that you, like Job, may encounter God. When you have finished your prayer, read Job 42:1–6 and compare your reaction to Job's.

Chapter

17

For Love
Is
Strong
as
Death

Song of Songs 8:5–14

Many Waters Cannot Quench Love

Who is that coming up from the wilderness,
    leaning upon her beloved?
Under the apple tree I awakened you.
There your mother was in labor with you;
    there she who bore you was in labor.
Set me as a seal upon your heart,
    as a seal upon your arm;
for love is strong as death,
    passion fierce as the grave.
Its flashes are flashes of fire,
    a raging flame.
Many waters cannot quench love,
    neither can floods drown it.
If one offered for love
    all the wealth of his house,
    it would be utterly scorned.
      (8:5–7)

They are together at last. The bride and the bridegroom have come out of the wilderness. They have survived their enforced separation, but now that is in the past. Under the apple tree, where the groom had been born, the two will celebrate their love.

Gone, too, is the cautionary note about love that the bride has repeatedly sounded to the daughters of Jerusalem. It is not that she has suddenly decided that love is not a force too powerful to control. Indeed the images of love's power over them are, if anything, strengthened in this passage.

Love's power is compared to that of death, a power no human being can escape. Love is as strong, as implacable as death. Like death, we have no power to resist love's call. The fierceness of passion is compared to the grave. The bride is paying tribute to its awe-full power.

Flashes of love are like flames, bright and burning. But even the flame image does not get to the heart of the real power of love. Passion is more like a raging inferno, whose heat sets all around it on fire. Such a fire cannot easily be quenched. Many waters cannot put out such a blaze. Even a flood would leave the fire untouched. Love, according to the bride, cannot be put out. Love, therefore, is the strongest power there is.

In spite of that frightening imagery, the bride exults in love. Love has captured her, and like the burning bush, she is on fire without being consumed. Nothing else matters except the fire of love burning so brightly within her. All that had once seemed important now becomes a matter of indifference. Wealth and position are of little account; they are to be scorned. Only love endures.

That is the ultimate aim of God's pursuit of us. God wants to set us on fire with the burning power of God's love. That transformation is not always easy. Sometimes it is frightening. We may be scared by the intensity of God's desire for us. We may be afraid of our growing desire for God. We may, like the bride, want to sound cautionary warnings. We may want to slow the process down, to make sure we are safe. We may want to hold onto other things that have given us a sense of security.

God, however, wants to sweep us off our feet and blow the embers of our love into a raging inferno, so that we can proclaim along with the bride that many waters cannot quench our love.

What Shall We Do for Our Sister?

We have a little sister,
    and she has no breasts.
What shall we do for our sister,

> on the day when she is spoken for?
> If she is a wall,
>> we will build upon her a battlement of silver;
> but if she is a door,
>> we will enclose her with boards of cedar.
>> *(8:8–9)*

Just as all seems to be resolved, the brothers, the keepers of propriety, enter the picture once again. The two lovers have just found each other. They are ready to commence their life together. The brothers, however, have the responsibility to protect the woman until she is ready for marriage, and in their eyes, she is not yet ready.

They still see her as a young child, a prepubescent. They do not yet see the development that marked her transition to mature womanhood. They are concerned, therefore, with making sure that no men have access to her until the proper time. They want to protect her "walls" so that they cannot be breached by an importunate lover. They want to nail up her door, so that no one may enter. They are convinced that in doing so, they are fulfilling their duty.

They have yet to deal with the development that has happened in the course of the book. She is no longer a child whom they can send out to take care of their vineyards. She is a mature woman, as attested by the description of the groom. She no longer needs their protection, but they are reluctant to relinquish their guard duty.

As we grow in our relationship with God, we may "outgrow" people and practices that have strengthened and protected us in the earlier stages of faith development. We may find that certain types of prayers no longer have the meaning and power they once did. People who have been influential in our growing faith in the past may no longer understand or even approve of the way in which our relationship is developing. Like the brothers, they may try to pull us back into a position of safety. They may reinforce our walls and try to board up our doors. Love, however, is not about safety; it is about being open and available to our Lover.

Make Haste, My Beloved

> I was a wall,
>   and my breasts were like towers;
> then I was in his eyes
>   as one who brings peace.
> Solomon had a vineyard at Baal-hamon;
>   he entrusted the vineyard to keepers;
>   each one was to bring for its fruit a thousand
>   pieces of silver.
> My vineyard, my very own, is for myself;
>   you, O Solomon, may have the thousand,
>   and the keepers of the fruit two hundred!
> O you who dwell in the gardens,
>   my companions are listening for your voice;
>   let me hear it.
> Make haste, my beloved,
>   and be like a gazelle
> or a young stag
>   upon the mountains of spices!
>   *(8:10–14)*

No more will the bride allow others to decide; she is ready to decide for herself. She is not a child under the guardianship of others. She is not a girl with no breasts, but a woman with breasts like towers.

They do not have to worry about keeping her safe for marriage, for she has already promised herself to the one she loves. It is she who will decide who it is that enters her garden, not her brothers. In fact, her lover is already present there, though the brothers do not know it. She bids her beloved, the one who dwells in her garden, to speak so that her companions are aware that she is no longer alone!

She is impatient for the fulfillment of their love. Make haste, my beloved, the bride calls out. She has waited so long, and the flames of her desire have been fanned into a roaring inferno. Like a young stag, he is to climb the last mountain, the mountain of their love, the mountain of spices. At that point the story ends, and we are left to imagine what comes next. The lover and the beloved have at last found each other, and no barriers are left.

All courtship is preparation for what lies ahead. The Song of Songs is a description, not of spiritual marriage, but of spiritual courtship. Union with God is not the end, according to the mystics, but the beginning of a whole new way of being in God, where the two really become one.

There is a deep longing within us for such union, for we are made for precisely that. As the story of the bride shows, it comes with great joy, but not without difficulty, fear, or frustration.

I do believe that God wants us, each and every one of us, as deeply and passionately as the groom in the story wants the bride. God is waiting for us to awake to our passion for God, and for that passion to blaze into a roaring inferno—for only in love will this marriage be consummated.

Journal Questions

1. Think of times when you have been overcome with strong passion. How did it make you feel? What was it that engaged your passion? Have any of those times been with God?

2. Make a list of people who have been important to your faith development in the past. What gifts have each offered to you? Have you left any relationships behind as you continued your spiritual journey? Was something in that relationship trying to hold you back, to keep you safe?

3. Marriage is a traditional image for the union of the soul with God. What is your image of marriage? Is it a helpful image for you? What kinds of issues does it raise?

Suggestions for Prayer

1. Slowly read chapter 8, verses 5–7. As you read, notice the images or words that catch your attention. Spend some time meditating on what God might be saying to you through this passage.

2. Pray that God may blow the embers of your love into a raging inferno. Spend some time in silence being aware of your love for God.

3. Make a list of all the people who have been important to you in your spiritual journey. Thank God for each of them by name and by the gifts they have given you. Ask God to continue to give you people who will nurture your love for God.

4. Spend time in praise of your Beloved.

18

*Passion
and
Prayer*

Reading the Song is like making love in that there needs to be respect for mystery and allure and the arresting of any conquering impulse.[50]

Praying the Song of Songs

I found that as I read the Song of Songs, and more important, as I prayed the Song, something happened.

Something happened in the way I view God. My understanding of God softened and deepened. A harsh, demanding God is not compatible with the images in the Song. Gone are the threats and the coercive power of God. In the Song God chooses invitation. I found an alluring and mysterious God, one who called me to leave all else and simply enjoy being with God. The portrait of God is one of mystery. The Groom comes and goes as God wills.

Something happened in the way I view myself as well. It took a while before I could think of myself in the terms of the bride in the Song. It was hard to believe that I could be as beautiful, as alluring, as compelling, and as dangerous to God as the bride seems to be to the groom. Yet over and over, I would hear the voice of God in the words of the Song. It is a mystery why God loves us the way God does, but that is the message of the Song of Songs. God loves us, and in so doing, chooses to be vulnerable.

Most important of all, something happened in my relationship with God. It helped me learn to love God better, and in learning to love God better, all kinds of things happened. It allowed me to risk falling in love.

I wish I could say that falling in love solved all my problems, but that has not happened. I wish I could say that I am never angry or frightened or anxious or sad, but that also is not true. Being in love does not exclude the darker emotions; in fact, I think that sometimes it sharpens their impact. Being in love, however, puts them all in context. It changes our priorities. It reminds us that we are not in this alone. Most of all, it creates a whole new way of looking at our lives and our world. It opens up a whole new set of possibilities.

In John of the Cross's understanding of spiritual life and growth, the Song of Songs describes that time of spiritual growth known as spiritual betrothal. It is analogous to falling in love in human terms. It is a time of great highs and great lows in the spiritual life. The lover finds ecstasy in the presence of the Beloved and agony in the Beloved's absence. All feelings are magnified, and the world around is transfused with a glow.

Few people are able to stay in a state of emotional intoxication permanently, in either their human relationships or their relationships with God. It is too exhausting, too all-consuming. Either the relationship dies or it moves on to a new level of intimacy and connection. The next level, according to John of the Cross, is spiritual marriage. Spiritual marriage shares with human marriage a lessening of the emotional highs and lows, and is characterized by a more constant sense of presence and union.

> It remains for the Spouse to make mention of the said Spiritual Marriage between the soul aforementioned and the Son of God, her Spouse, which is far greater than the Betrothal because it is a total transformation in the Beloved (and thus I think that this estate is never without confirmation in grace, because the faithfulness of both is confirmed, that of the soul being confirmed in God) wherein on either side there is made surrender by total possession, of the one to the other in consummate union of love, as far as may be in this life, wherein the soul is made Divine and becomes God by participation, in so far as may be in this life, and thus this is the highest estate which in this life is attainable.[51]

In many marriage services is a prayer that the two may become one. In spiritual marriage, that is the intent as well: all distinctions and all barriers are dissolved. There is no longer any separation between the lovers. "[T]he soul is dissolved in that transformation wherein, inflamed and changed in love, it was annihilated and undone as to all that which was not love, and left so that it knew naught else save love."[52] In doing that we become more fully the people we were created to be.

We are meant for such an intimate relationship with our Lover. We may never reach the perfection of spiritual marriage in this life, any more than we manage perfection in our earthly marriages. It is, however, an ideal toward which we long. In the meantime we live as best we can, praying that we may continue to grow in love of our Beloved and that one day we may be fully united with God.

Walsh claims that "the intimacy of God is something maybe only a mystic can bear." I believe, however, that such intimacy, as difficult as it may be for humans, is God's call to each and every one of us. God wants to be in that kind of love relationship with us. We may not ever do it perfectly in this life. At times, we may mess it up completely, but the call is still there. Our Beloved continues to call us to come away, and someday we may dare to leave everything behind and follow.

Passion for God

We can imagine God in many different ways. We can relate to God in many different ways. We can see God as an all-protective Father. We can imagine God as a stern lawgiver. We can imagine God as a lofty figure, unconcerned with petty human beings. We can see God as a hard-to-please authority figure. We can imagine God as a "hanging judge" or a Santa Claus or a fairy godmother. We can imagine God as a clockmaker who set all into motion and has no further interaction with creation. All those images have been used to think about God.

Why then should we use the image of God as Lover? What does that image reveal about God (and ourselves) that other images do not? It captures, I think, the yearning every person has to rejoin with the One who created us. It speaks to us of our deepest desire, a desire so deep that at times we are completely unaware of it. According to Walsh, "Still, the search and desire, the giving of one's heart, soul, and might to God remain the faithful person's truest yearnings. This woman's [the bride in the Song of Songs] journey for a union where she can give her all in love imitates, on the sexual level, the spiritual quest for God."[53] Our deepest desire is for that union with the One who is the source of all life and love.

For me, the image that has drawn me closest to God has been the image of the Beloved. It speaks to me of relationship and journey. It deals with the themes of absence and presence, joy and pain. Most of all it has called me, and continues to call me, to grow in my love of God until I have been completely transformed, and I and my Beloved are one. In Christian theology we are called to become one with Christ, and that image has enormous potential to transform. "Perhaps only the person who knows how to give himself completely, body and soul, to another can worship God with his total being."[54] It is this giving that the Song of Songs celebrates.

Equality with God

The bride and the groom in the Song of Songs have an extraordinary relationship of equality. Both sing praises of the other. Both give themselves to the other. Both claim that the other has captured them. Both are vulnerable.

In most traditions the idea of equality with our Creator seems unthinkable. If we are to use the Song of Songs for prayer, imagining ourselves as brides and God as the groom, what do we do with the notion of equality that is portrayed in the Song? How and in what way do we consider ourselves equals with God?

It is a troublesome question. The easiest way to get equality is to try to lower God to our level. Attempts have been made through the centuries to view God as either powerless or subject somehow to our control. In that case, however, God is no longer God. What point is there in having any special relationship with God if God is no more than we are?

If we cannot lower God to our level, and if equality is necessary for a real relationship of love, then the only possibility is for God to raise us to God's level. How could that be, since we are mortal and God is immortal? Many would claim that any such relationship between two very different beings is impossible. Some would deny even the possibility of divine-human love; the gulf between God and human is too deep to be bridged. Others despair of our ever being able to bridge the gulf between God and ourselves. Bernard of Clairvaux deals directly with that issue. According to him, love creates its own sense of equality.

> Nor is it to be feared that inequality between the persons will prevent this coming together in one will, for love knows nothing of such distance. It is loving, not paying respect, that gives love its name. Let someone else be horrified, stupefied, terrified, amazed; he who loves feels nothing of these. His love fills him; love takes all other affections captive when it comes. Therefore what it loves it loves, and it knows nothing else. He who is feared, honored, regarded with awe, and admired would rather be loved. They are bride and Bridegroom. What other bond and commitment do you seek to find between those who are betrothed than to love and be loved?[55]

If equality is necessary for the love relationship, it is equally true that love makes such equality possible. Only love gives us the courage to give ourselves fully to God. Only love allows us to presume to enter into relationship with God. Only love allows us to express our passion toward One who is in every other way beyond our reach.

As we give ourselves in love, so God is giving God's self to us. As the lovers completely give themselves to each other, the line between bride and groom dissolves, and the two become one. At that point they are equal, for they are one. So it is with God and us as well. As mutual giving between a person and God continues, the two become indistinguishable. "The reason for this is that in the union and transformation of love the one gives possession of itself to the other, and each one gives and abandons itself to the other and exchanges itself for the other."[56]

Is such equality really possible? According to the mystics, it happens when we completely give ourselves to our Beloved, for then we will be "so alike that one is transfigured into the other."[57] Although complete equality may not occur in this life, I believe, along with lovers of God throughout the centuries, that we can get glimpses of that possibility, and that we can come ever closer to that equality. It is not a quest for the fainthearted. Perhaps only lovers like those in the Song would dare to risk so much. It takes a certain fool-heartedness to fall head over heels in love, especially with God.

Passionate Prayer

When I was first drawn to the Song of Songs, I had no idea where my prayer would lead me. Although I knew in a vague way what was in it, it had not really touched my life. It had not been a part of the Bible that I had previously studied.

I believe that if anyone reads, really reads the Bible with an openness to hear what is being said, they will be transformed. In my tradition that is what is meant when we call the Bible the "word of God." We affirm our belief that God still speaks to us through those words written so many years ago.

Although I would have agreed, in principle, that any part of the Bible could speak to me, I would not have guessed the profound affect the Song of Songs would have on me, on my prayer life, and ultimately on my relationship with God.

Different parts of the Bible show us different sides, different facets of God. When I felt called to deeply engage the Song of Songs, I was transfixed by a passionate side of God that I had not previously experienced in that intensity. In experiencing it, I discovered my own hidden passion for God. I fell in love with God in a way that I had never done before.

My hope in writing this book is that others might have the opportunity to experience the passion and the love that have become so important to me. May you grow in your love of God, and may your prayer be passionate, this day and always.

ENDNOTES

CHAPTER 1 *Introduction*

1. Janet K. Ruffing, *Spiritual Direction: Beyond the Beginnings* (Mahwah, NJ: Paulist Press, 2000), p. 115.
2. John of the Cross, *Selected Writings,* ed. Kieran Kavanaugh, The Classics of Western Spirituality (Mahwah, NJ: Paulist Press, 1987), p. 219.

CHAPTER 2 *Praying with the Song of Songs Through the Ages*

3. Origen, *The Song of Songs: Commentary and Homilies,* trans. and anno. R. P. Lawson, *Ancient Christian Writers,* vol. 26 (Westminster, MD: Newman Press, 1957), p. 23.
4. Madeleine L'Engle, *The Rock That Is Higher: Story as Truth* (Wheaton, IL: Harold Shaw Publishers, 1993), p. 257.
5. Carey Ellen Walsh, *Exquisite Desire: Religion, the Erotic, and the Song of Songs* (Minneapolis: Fortress Press, 2000), p. 51.
6. Lawrence Boadt, ed., *The Song of Solomon: Love Poetry of the Spirit* (New York: St. Martin's Press, 1999), p. 11.
7. Walsh, p. xiii.
8. Ibid., p. 30.
9. *The People's Bible: Song of Songs,* trans. Sidney Brichto (London: Sinclair-Stevenson, 2000), p. 4.
10. Walsh, p. 191.
11. Ariel Bloch and Chana Bloch, *The Song of Songs* (New York: Random House, 1995), p. 32.
12. Origen, p. 44.
13. Ibid., p. 10.
14. Ibid., p. 15.
15. Ibid., p. 129.
16. R. P. Lawson, foreword to Origen, *The Song of Songs: Commentary and Homilies* (Westminster, MD: Newman Press, 1957), p. 14.
17. Origen, p. 64.
18. Ibid., p. 21.
19. Bernard of Clairvaux, *Selected Works,* trans. and foreword G. R. Evans, The Classics of Western Spirituality (Mahwah, NJ: Paulist Press, 1978), p. 212.

20. Ibid., p. 239.
21. Ibid., p. 277.
22. John of the Cross, *Selected Writings,* p. 229.
23. Raymond Jacques Tournay, *Word of God, Song of Love: A Commentary on the Song of Songs,* trans. J. Edward Crowley (Mahwah, NJ: Paulist Press, 1988), p. 166.
24. *The People's Bible,* p. 5.
25. Bloch and Bloch, p. 35.
26. *The Song of Songs: A New Translation,* trans. Marcia Falk (San Francisco: HarperSanFrancisco, 1993), p. xvii.
27. Walsh, p. 8.
28. Rumi, *The Essential Rumi,* trans. Coleman Barks with John Moyne, A. J. Arberry, and Reynold Nicholson (San Francisco: HarperSanFrancisco, 1995), p. 229.
29. Ruffing, p. 133.

CHAPTER 3   *Let Him Kiss Me (1:1–8)*

30. Bernard of Clairvaux, pp. 214–5.

CHAPTER 4   *A Mare Among Pharaoh's Chariots*

31. *The Song of Songs,* p. xxii.
32. Ibid., section 4.
33. Ann Koepke, *Herbs and Flowers in the Bible* (Cincinnati: Forward Movement Publications, 1990), p. 8.

CHAPTER 5   *His Intention Toward Me Was Love*

34. Eugene H. Peterson, *The Message: The Wisdom Books* (Colorado Springs, CO: Navpress Publishing Group, 1996), p. 379.
35. Bloch and Bloch, p. 57.
36. *The Song of Songs,* section 8.

CHAPTER 6   *Come Away*

37. Bloch and Bloch, p. 155.
38. Ibid.
39. Tournay, p. 91.
40. Walsh, p. 80.
41. Bloch and Bloch, p. 157.

CHAPTER 7   *I Sought Him Whom My Soul Loves*

42. *The Song of Songs,* section 8.

CHAPTER 8   *Daughters of Jerusalem, Come Out*

43. *The People's Bible,* p. 6.
44. George L. Scheper, "Pomegranate," in Lawrence Boadt, ed., *The Song of Solomon,* p. 36.
45. Walsh, p. 97.

CHAPTER 10   *You Have Ravished My Heart*

46. Walsh, p. 70.
47. Bloch and Bloch, p. 177.

CHAPTER 14   *My Perfect One*

48. Bloch and Bloch, p. 188.

CHAPTER 16   *There I Will Give You My Love*

49. Bloch and Bloch, p. 208.

CHAPTER 18   *Passion and Prayer*

50. Walsh, p. 52.
51. John of the Cross, *The Complete Works of Saint John of the Cross, Doctor of the Church,* vol. 12: *Spiritual Canticle,* trans. and ed. E. Allison Peers (Westminster, MD: Newman Press, 1964), p. 133.
52. Ibid., p. 101.
53. Walsh, p. 139.
54. *The People's Bible,* p. 5.
55. Bernard of Clairvaux, pp. 271–2.
56. John of the Cross, *Complete Works,* p. 65.
57. John of the Cross, *Selected Writings,* p. 235

SELECTED BIBLIOGRAPHY

Bernard of Clairvaux. *Selected Works*. Translated by G. R. Evans. The Classics of Western Spirituality. Mahwah, NJ: Paulist Press, 1978.

Bloch, Ariel, and Chana Bloch. *The Song of Songs*. New York: Random House, 1995.

Boadt, Lawrence, ed. and intro. *The Song of Solomon: Love Poetry of the Spirit*. New York: St. Martin's Press, 1999.

John of the Cross. *The Complete Works of Saint John of the Cross, Doctor of the Church*, vol. 2. Translated and edited by E. Allison Peers. Westminster, MD: Newman Press, 1964.

John of the Cross. *Selected Writings*. Edited by Kieran Kavanaugh. The Classics of Western Spirituality. Mahwah, NJ: Paulist Press, 1987.

Koepke, Ann. *Herbs and Flowers in the Bible*. Cincinnati: Forward Movement Publications, 1990.

L'Engle, Madeleine. *The Rock That Is Higher: Story as Truth*. Wheaton, IL: Harold Shaw Publishers, 1993.

Origen. *The Song of Songs: Commentary and Homilies*. Translated and annotated by R. P. Lawson. Ancient Christian Writers, vol. 26. Westminster, MD: Newman Press, 1957.

The People's Bible: Song of Songs. Translated by Sidney Brichto. London: Sinclair-Stevenson, 2000 Mahwah, NJ: Paulist Press, 2000.

Rumi. *The Essential Rumi*. Translated by Coleman Barks with John Moyne, A.J. Arberry, and Reynold Nicholson. San Francisco: HarperSanFrancisco, 1995.

Falk, Marcia. *The Song of Songs: A New Translation and Interpretation*. San Francisco: HarperSanFrancisco, 1993.

Tournay, Raymond Jacques. *Word of God, Song of Love: A Commentary on the Song of Songs*. Translated by J. Edward Crowley. Mahwah, NJ: Paulist Press, 1988.

Walsh, Carey Ellen. *Exquisite Desire: Religion, the Erotic, and the Song of Songs*. Minneapolis: Fortress Press, 2000.